Cooking with
HERBS &
SPICES

Cooking with
HERBS & SPICES

Monica Mawson

HAMLYN
LONDON · NEW YORK · SYDNEY · TORONTO

Acknowledgements

The author and publishers would like to thank the
following for their help and co-operation in supplying
colour pictures for this book:
American Long-Grain Rice: pages 44/45, 55, 56/57,
58, 67, 82
British Bacon Bureau: page 46
British Egg Information Service: pages 102/103
British Sausage Bureau: pages 43, 79, 80/81
Danish Food Centre, London: pages 32/33
Frank Cooper's Preserves: page 101
Mushroom Growers' Association: pages 34, 91
New Zealand Lamb Information Bureau: pages 31,
68/69
Pannett and Neden (L. Noel and Sons): page 22
Pasta Information Centre: pages 70, 92

First published in 1970 under the title *Hamlyn's Guide
to Herbs and Spices*
Second edition published in 1972 under the title *Herb
and Spice Cookery*
Reprinted in 1973
Third edition published in 1978 by the
Hamlyn Publishing Group Limited
London · New York · Sydney · Toronto
Astronaut House, Feltham, Middlesex, England
© Copyright The Hamlyn Publishing Group Limited 1978
Reprinted in 1979

ISBN 0 600 34567 X

Line illustrations by Marilyn Day
Printed in Hong Kong

Contents

Introduction

The use of herbs and spices is often taken for granted, but only a little thought is required to realise that the selection and addition of these many subtle flavours supply the individuality which cooking must possess. After all, the thousands of available recipes are only guidelines. The judicious addition of herbs and spices stamps an original image upon dishes not only of your own creation but also those prepared from the stereotyped convenience foods of today.

Their ability to offer you such variety in your cooking is also coupled with another wonderful attribute — they take little shelf room in your kitchen or freezer, and need only minor growing areas in your garden. In window boxes and pots they can be very decorative as well as serving a useful function.

My research into this fascinating subject was a revelation in itself. For today we are indebted to some of our Roman invaders who had the forethought to bring over many of the herbs which we now enjoy. Some can still be found growing wild in our countryside — chervil, fennel, oregano and sweet cicely, to mention but a few — remaining as silent sentinels to the romance and history of our country.

The intrepid explorer, Marco Polo, was the first man to set the West afire with desire for the spices of the East, then commanding fantastic sums.

Herbs and spices are indeed intriguing, and as you get to know them more intimately they will give you more and more enjoyment.

Monica Mawson

The History of the Herbalist

The art and superstitions of herbalists must be as old as time itself. Genesis I, verse 11 tells us, 'And God said, Let the earth bring forth grass, the herb yielding seed, and the fruit tree yielding fruit after his kind, whose seed is in itself, upon the earth: and it was so.' And verse 29 says, 'And God said, Behold, I have given you every herb bearing seed, which is upon the face of all the earth.' Since then trees, herbs and flowers have all played a great part, for good and evil, in the history of mankind.

From the beginning man had an affinity with living plants, for it was on them, together with the meat of wild animals, that he largely depended for his food. Through trial and error, he learned which were poisonous, which were nourishing and good to eat, and which had healing properties.

The first and greatest true medical doctor of all time, known as 'The Father of Medicine', was the Greek, Hippocrates (460–377 BC), part of whose code of medical ethics exists even today as the 'Hippocratic oath' taken by medical graduates. He was certainly learned on the subject of herbs, since he left a list of some four hundred 'simples' (herbs used medicinally). Following him, Theophrastus of Athens (372–287 BC), a pupil of Aristotle, was one of the most important contributors to ancient botanical science. He wrote the earliest work in existence on the subject — his ten volume *History of Plants*.

In China, India and Egypt the early works on medicines and herbs from the 4th century BC are known to have been of a high order. Before this era, the knowledge of medicine possessed by the ancient Egyptians, Babylonians, Assyrians, Sumerians and others was extensive, but it can now only be judged through excavations, engravings and inscriptions on stone and clay.

The Greek physician, Pedacius Dioscorides, said to have been the private physician of Antony and Cleopatra, left early in the 1st century AD what may be regarded as the earliest herbal in existence. His compilation of six hundred or so plants remained the source of herbal therapy for many centuries thereafter.

The monks had special herb gardens at their monasteries, where they grew herbs for treating illness and healing wounds. The Benedictine order at Monte Cassino in the 8th century was possibly one of the first, followed by most of the large monasteries and convents, although physic gardens are known to have been cultivated in France and in England under the Romans. The first public herb gardens, however, were founded in Padua in 1533.

The monks also learned to use herbs in other ways. Everyone has heard of, if not actually enjoyed, the famous Chartreuse liqueur made by the Carthusian monks, but it is only one of numerous liqueurs distilled at various monasteries.

In England, Alfred the Great (AD 849–899) was known to have used a 'Leech Book' which listed some five hundred healing herbs. William Turner, between 1551 and 1568, was the first man to publish a herbal in English (before that time herbal books had been written in Latin, German and Italian) listing plants alphabetically, and also for the first time recording their origins.

But it was John Gerard, the English herbalist and surgeon, who in 1597 was the first to produce a really comprehensive and profound book on herbs and their properties. His great 'Herball' was fully illustrated and gave details of each plant including its origin, history, use, methods of planting and the best type of soil for each.

Like other apothecaries of his time, Gerard had a garden on the banks of the River Fleet in the City of London where he grew and studied plants. He was also apothecary to James I, during whose reign the Worshipful Company of Apothecaries founded their famous Physic Garden.

It should be mentioned that Gerard's name might not have become so famous had not another London apothecary, Thomas Johnson (who had his own garden at Snow Hill), re-illustrated, re-edited and re-issued Gerard's book in 1633, twenty-one years after his death. Nevertheless, it was Gerard who inspired every writer on herbs thereafter. And there have been many.

Nicholas Culpeper (1616–1654) was both an astrologer and a physician, and in his various books on herbals he grouped plants by astrological influence. He also tried to surround with magic and mystery the old art of healing with 'simples'. This brought him into conflict with the medical practitioners of his time and also brought the practice of herbal cures into disrepute.

The 17th century saw the height of the use of

herbals for curative medicine, famous physic gardens growing as many as sixteen hundred different plants.

But with the advance of scientific knowledge, medicine developed beyond the use of the natural properties of pure plants, which through the preceding centuries had been the only means whereby physicians could help their patients. Synthetic substances were then evolved which contained the active principles of the drugs previously found only in nature, and others were invented from entirely new substances. Thus the use of pure herbs and plants began to decline, and plants were grown for the beauty of their flowers alone.

Herbs and spices, however, are now enjoying a big revival as more and more people become interested in them, largely in the culinary field. This is probably because, as travel becomes more universal, the thrill of tasting the exciting flavours of foods of different countries is being experienced with such pleasure by so many people that the joy of reproducing the dishes at home is greatly increasing sales of herbs and spices. And let us not forget that the forefathers of the British used dozens of herbs and spices in their dishes and took many of these with them when they emigrated to the New World to found the North American cuisine (which now uses some spices with lavish abandon).

In some cases the use of herbs and plants in the medical field is being revived (or perhaps the practice has never died out). After all, penicillin, that wonderful drug which opened up a whole new vista for curative antibiotics, was discovered and grown from natural plant-mould on melon.

In November 1955, when Queen Elizabeth II visited the Royal London Homoeopathic Hospital (of which she is patron), she was presented with a beautifully arranged bouquet of forty-two flowers, leaves and berries used today in homoeopathic medicine.

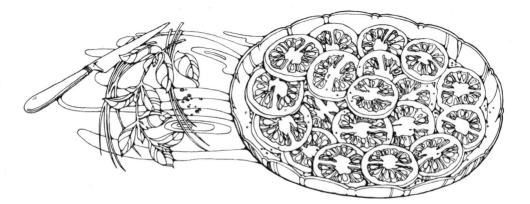

Legends, Fables and Witchcraft

The facts and fables of plant life in all its aspects are inextricably interwoven. At some moment in his evolution man must have begun to ponder upon the strange phenomena of trees, shrubs and plants which lose their leaves and therefore seemingly their life in winter, yet come to life again in the spring, whilst others remain green all through the year. These observations, among others, probably led to the belief that there were gods from whom life itself springs.

In less enlightened past centuries, placating these gods for the well-being of life-giving crops was all-important to superstitious man. Gradually seasonal festivals were inaugurated to propitiate the gods for their favours in different seasons, particularly the all-important season of fertility in the spring.

Horrible human sacrifices were perpetrated to this end. As plants were vital to the life of man, it was held that they must be equally necessary to the gods. Thus different plants became associated with ritual ceremonies for the worship of each celestial being.

Witches played a great part in the superstitions of the past. Are we not all, even now, guilty of some superstitious practices ourselves, though we may not be aware of them? Witches relied heavily upon natural plant life for their armoury of magic and potions — for example, their well-known escapade of flying on broomsticks. The broomstick was certainly made from one of the witch's special trees, either elder or hawthorn.

Some of the earliest associations with magic took the form of poisons and their antidotes, meted out by witches and sorcerers in every part of the world. About 4500 BC, Gula, the Sumerian goddess of sorcery, became the earliest deity connected with such evil doings. In ancient Greek and Roman legends Hecate was the sorceress who discovered poison and, with her daughters Medea and Circe, practised every kind of wickedness with poisonous concoctions made from plants.

The early Caesars seem to have taken to this practice enthusiastically. They poisoned anyone who got in their way or whom they disliked, or even just for the fun of it — often ordering their own physician to administer it!

In the East, the Chinese and Hindus were masters at concocting and administering poisons, although theirs were more often made from animals than solely from plants. Aconite root, opium, mandrake, belladonna and hemlock were the plants most commonly used for poison potions.

During the Renaissance poisoning was a common method of removing an enemy or an unwanted mistress or lover. In Europe, Italy led the field in the art of poisoning and sold poisons and the recipes for them to other nations. So great was the fear of being poisoned that, in the 16th and 17th centuries, rich households employed special wine and food tasters who tasted each goblet of wine or dish of food before their masters would touch it.

Probably a witch's most valuable single aid was a mandrake (*Mandragora officinarum*), undoubtedly the plant with the most evil reputation. The Arabs call it 'the devil's testicles'. It was said to shriek when pulled from the ground and to kill any human who attempted to dig it up, so it was hauled out on ropes by a dog which was tethered to a tree. It often looked like a man with long legs so was frequently included in love-potions as an aphrodisiac and to facilitate pregnancy.

Mandrake was used in the East as a narcotic, and Pliny the Elder (1st century BC) also mentioned it as a sort of anaesthetic to cause insensitivity in people undergoing operations. If too much was eaten or if it was eaten with pickles, it was said to send a man mad. Obviously it had every charm for a witch!

Witches and later apothecaries were also much in demand through the ages to produce aphrodisiacs and love-potions. At one time the Greeks and Romans used a mixture of pepper, myrrh, perfume and magic as an aphrodisiac and drank the mixture out of scented earthenware goblets. Glands of pigs, horses, hyenas and other animals were another favourite mixture. Winged ants, Spanish fly and later ambergris were all favoured to promote amorous passions. But the list of ingredients for love-potions was legion. Each period and each country had its popular combinations and, of course, mixed them with magical spells.

When the Christian Church became powerful it tried to eradicate the evil practices of the Druids and ordered their sacred groves to be cut down and burned, often building a church on the site. Heavy penalties were imposed upon anyone practising the revolting cult of black magic, with its direct affiliation with the devil and its superstitious practices involving plants and flowers.

A herb with a turbulent history of love and passion is basil. It is said that Salome hid the head of John the Baptist in a pot of basil. It seems a popular herb in which to keep heads of murdered men: in Keats' poem 'Isabella, or the Pot of Basil', Isabella keeps the head of her murdered lover in a pot of basil and waters it with her tears.

On the other hand, in Italy a sprig of basil worn by a young man when calling on his girlfriend shows his intentions are serious. It is also supposed to die instantly if the wearer be 'light of love' (I have heard that about any flower!). In the East basil is a talisman against witchcraft.

The list of good, protective plants is headed by angelica. Even the down-to-earth, unsuperstitious Gerard admits that angelica is efficacious against witchcraft. Legend has it that its virtues were first revealed to a monk, and so it became known as the 'Holy Ghost plant'. At all events, in the early herbals angelica, particularly its root, was described as having more medicinal uses than any other plant. The root was a remarkable remedy against poison, the plague and the bite of a mad dog, and it seemed to help every part of the system from heart to spleen.

The bay tree is another talisman against destruction. The old saying 'Neither witch nor devil, thunder nor lightning will hurt a man in the place where a bay tree is' means that it would be a wise precaution to plant a bay tree in the garden. And to prove the point, that great Roman statesman, the Emperor Tiberius, was said to have been so terrified of thunder that when a storm raged he crawled under his bed and covered his head with bay leaves!

Of course, the bay tree must be special, because mythology states that the nymph Daphne was turned into a bay tree to save her from the pursuit of the god Apollo, after which the bay tree naturally was Apollo's favourite tree.

Garlic is another plant which seems not only good for health but also a powerful antidote to poison. The Greek god Hermes is said to have taught the hero Odysseus to counteract the potions of Circe, daughter of sorceress Hecate, with garlic. Dioscorides, private physician to Antony and Cleopatra, praised garlic amongst other herbs for its healing virtues.

Theophrastus and Aristotle mention that the men who went to cut dangerous plants and gather precious roots, so much prized in that day, rubbed themselves with oil or consumed large quantities of garlic as a protection. And so the story repeats itself to the present day. There must surely be something in the theory — what a pity it has *that* odour!

Herbs and How to Grow Them

The letter against each herb denotes its type of lifespan (A for annual, B for biennial, P for perennial).

Angelica *Angelica archangelica* and *sylvestris,* B or short-lived P. There are two types of angelica, *sylvestris* being the wild variety. Usually only the cultivated angelica, which has thick, hollow, light green stems, is used for culinary purposes as it is far superior in flavour and tenderness.

Angelica can grow up to 2.5 m/8 feet in height and 1.5 m/5 feet across, so takes up a lot of room; it should therefore be grown at the back of a border. In any case, it likes a rich damp soil with a good deal of shade.

The seeds must be really fresh or they will not germinate, so sow directly they are ripe. The plant also seeds itself freely if the flower head is left on to ripen. In this case the plant will live for only two years, dying after it has flowered, but if the flower heads are cut off as soon as they appear the plant will continue for three to four years or more.

The most popular use for angelica is to candy the stems for decoration and flavour, but all of the plant can be used, including the young leaf stalks and shoots, to sweeten tart fruits such as gooseberries and blackcurrants for stewing. The recommended proportion is about 25 g/1 oz of fresh angelica to each 225 g/8 oz of fruit. The leaves and stems can also be used to flavour orange marmalade and for making a herbal tea or infusion said to aid the digestion.

The whole plant is used as a vegetable in some countries and various parts of it, from the roots to the seeds, are used in the making of such liquors as vermouth, gin, absinthe, Benedictine, etc.

Balm (Lemon Balm) *Melissa officinalis,* P. There are several types of balm, but only one for culinary herb cultivation—the common or lemon balm which grows to about 70 cm/2½ feet.

Balm is very easy to grow, either from seed planted in late spring or by dividing the roots in spring or autumn. In fact it is apt to become a nuisance, because the seeds will scatter and sow themselves rather too freely unless the flower heads are cut off; the roots creep as well, so they need watching. The plant should be cut right down in the autumn.

Lemon balm is a delight in the garden for the scent of its leaves when crushed, and bees (the name *Melissa* is derived from the Greek for bee) are inordinately fond of the nectar in the flowers. Beekeepers often rub the insides of their hives with the leaves to encourage the bees to stay at home.

The flavour of lemon is not as pronounced as the scent, so a fair quantity should be used. It also tends to lose its flavour with prolonged cooking, so add it only towards the end.

Balm is a good plant for growing in window boxes and pots. The leaves can be frozen or dried.

Basil (Sweet Basil) *Ocimum basilicum,* A. There are some 40 types of basil, but the two discussed here are those most easily grown for culinary use.

In warm countries basil grows as a perennial, but it is cut down immediately by frost so in cold climates must be treated as a half-hardy annual. It grows to about 60 cm/2 feet in height.

The seeds should not be sown outside until all fear of frost is past, but they may be started in a greenhouse in the warmth, then planted out in late spring in well drained soil in a sunny sheltered position. Once the plants have established themselves it is best to nip out the tops to make them bush out, and also to delay the flowering for as long as possible.

Basil is one of the most important herbs in cooking; use fresh whenever possible or dried in winter. It has a highly aromatic flavour and is used extensively in French, Greek and Italian cooking in which a tomato dish or sauce is seldom made without it.

It is an excellent plant for growing in window boxes and pots. The leaves freeze and dry well.

Bush Basil *Ocimum minimum,* A. This is a miniature variety which grows only 15-20 cm/6-8 inches high. It has a less robust growth with much smaller leaves than sweet basil and is grown mostly for decoration.

The flavour of the leaves is also very aromatic, and they are particularly good mixed with other herbs. The leaves can be frozen but are not usually dried.

Bay *Laurus nobilis,* P. Bay, known also as Sweet Bay or Bay Laurel, is one of the laurel family and the only one whose leaves may be used in cooking.

Angelica

Basil

Chervil

In warm climates the tree will grow up to 15-18 m/50-60 feet, but in more temperate climates it rarely exceeds 12 m/40 feet. However, this does not mean that it cannot be kept pruned to any height or shape desired.

The tree is an evergreen but does not like very hard frost, or worse still freezing winds. If grown in a tub it can be brought indoors or moved to shelter for the winter.

For an ornamental shape the main pruning should be done in April, then two or three times during the summer but not after September, although the leaves can be cut singly for using fresh at any time of the year. It is also better to use secateurs rather than shears, as they will not leave the foliage ragged and brown. Bay can be propagated by cuttings taken in late summer.

Bay leaves are an important flavour for cooking both savoury and sweet dishes, and they are an essential part of a bouquet garni. The leaves dry well.

Bergamot *Monarda*, P. A plant of the mint family, bergamot grows to 60-90 cm/2-3 feet. It has flowers varying in colour from white to bright red, which bees adore.

The red (didyma) is considered the best for scent and flavour. It can be grown from seed or by taking cuttings in July, but is usually propagated by root division in early spring.

The flowers and leaves make an unusual addition to salads and white wine cups, but are perhaps best known as herb teas or infusions, said to be an aid to relaxation. The leaves and flowers can be dried.

Bog Myrtle *Myrica gale*, P. As its name implies, this shrubby plant grows wild in bog areas, reaching from 60 cm-1.5 m/2-5 feet in height according to position. The fruit in particular produces a waxy substance from which candles were once made, hence its old nickname of Candle-berry. The fruit and leaves are slightly bitter but impart an unusual and delicious flavour to a stew. I dry and chop the leaves ready for use. The leaves dry well but are not suitable for freezing.

Borage *Borago officinalis*, A. Borage is an annual which grows to 45-60 cm/1½-2 feet and has clusters of lovely sky blue flowers. It seeds itself profusely,

and I have found seedlings growing some 27 m/30 yards from the original plant. Seeds can be sown deliberately from March to July.

Borage has a light cucumber flavour, and the leaves and flowers are an essential garnishing ingredient for summer cups such as Pimms, claret cups, etc. They can also be chopped for an addition to salads. The leaves do not dry well, but the flowers can be crystallised.

Burnet *Sanguisorba minor*, P. Also called Salad Burnet, this pretty leafed herb now grows wild in England, especially on the chalk downs of the south. It is easy to grow either from seed or from root division. It grows to about 30-38 cm/12-15 inches and the leaf stems spread out to cover an area of about 60 cm/2 feet, so when planting allow plenty of room.

The leaves have a slight flavour of cucumber so are good in salads, and when chopped make a compatible mixture with tarragon and rosemary in stews, sauces and cheese dishes. They are often included in herb vinegars and tisanes.

It is a useful herb to grow because the leaves do not die off and can be added to salads in winter, although I find the older leaves are apt to be a bit tough unless chopped finely. The leaves can be frozen but do not dry well.

Chervil *Anthriscus cerefolium*, A. Chervil is actually a hardy annual although almost a biennial; if the seeds are sown in late summer the leaves can be picked all through the winter, or it can be one of the first herbs for picking in the spring. Sown again in early spring it will give a continuous cycle through the summer and autumn.

Growing 45-60 cm/1½-2 feet, the feathery leaves are similar to a flat variety of parsley in appearance. In fact in France it is often used in place of parsley.

The leaves have a light anise flavour; chervil is one of the essential components of 'fines herbes' for omelettes, egg dishes, etc. It must be used fresh, or at least added after the cooking is completed, because the flavour is killed by boiling. The flavour is so delicate that it requires a quantity in each dish, so grow a considerable number of plants.

It is an ideal plant for window boxes and pots. The leaves can be frozen and dry well.

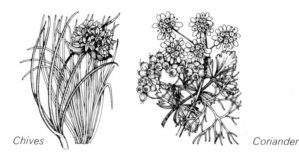

Chives

Coriander

Chives *Allium schoenoprasum*, P. There are two distinct types, one being the 'giant' which is larger than the other with grass-like leaves. The larger one is infinitely superior to my mind.

Chives are a hardy perennial growing up to about 30 cm/1 foot in height, and although they can be grown from seed planted in April it is much easier to start with a few 'bulbs'. These become matted together after a few years, when it is better to divide the clumps in early spring or autumn, keeping the outside bulblets and discarding the matted centres. They are one of the few herbs which like a fairly rich soil.

The flowers are a pretty mauve colour, growing like little pincushions on the end of each stem. If they are not to be used, or there are sufficient plants for both decorative and culinary use, cut some down to ground level as soon as the flowers appear. The leaves will start to grow again within a week and will remain green instead of dying off, as they are apt to do while the plant flowers.

Chives are unrivalled when used raw in salads and as a garnish for soups, sauces and over vegetables (cut into short lengths with a pair of scissors). In fact, chives and parsley are indispensable in any kitchen.

Chives are ideal for window boxes and pots and make a good border plant as well. The leaves freeze perfectly, but I do not recommend drying them, although it is possible to do so.

Coriander (Chinese or Japanese Parsley) *Coriandum sativum*, A. Coriander is usually thought of as a spice, since the seeds, both whole and ground, figure prominently in European, Middle Eastern, Eastern, and South American cooking and are one of the components of the mixed pickling spice we buy for home-made chutney.

It must be stressed, however, that the smell and taste of green coriander and that of the dried seeds are completely and utterly different. The leaves and green seed pods have an unpleasant odour, but both are used extensively in many countries — particularly in Indian curries. It would be unwise to allow the odour to put you off trying them, for mixed with other herbs and spices they can be delicious in many dishes. In Greece and Cyprus the leaves are much favoured as an addition to green salads; I personally found them overpowering, but this is merely a matter of taste.

The plants grow to about 60 cm/2 feet in height. Sow the seeds in early spring and cut down the plants as soon as the seeds show signs of ripening or they will drop quickly. Then hang the plants up to dry over a piece of cloth if the seeds are to be collected. The leaves can be frozen but are not satisfactory dried. The seeds dry well.

Costmary (Alecost or Bible Leaf) *Chrysanthem belsamita*, P. Costmary grows to about 90 cm/3 feet and dies down in the winter. It is best to buy or beg a small plant from a neighbour, as it creeps to nuisance proportions so should be watched and new shoots curtailed.

The leaves can be used sparingly in stews and soups, especially mixed with other herbs. Fresh or dried, the leaves are good for herbal teas or infusions. They were once used for flavouring home-brewed ale. The leaves can be frozen or dried.

Dill *Anethum graveolens*, A. Dill is a native of the Mediterranean and Black Sea areas. The leaves — or as they are called when dried, dill weed — have the faintest flavour of caraway, but seem to combine a slight sweetness with an aromatic sharpness. The seeds have a more pungent flavour.

Dill is known to be good for the digestion and dill water for babies is a byword. It is also famous the world over for pickling. Dill pickled cucumber is a favourite of many people and countries.

It is an annual which grows to a height of 75-90 cm/2½-3 feet. The seeds should be sown in early spring or summer where they are to remain, without fear of frost, as they dislike being moved. Thin out later, leaving 30 cm/12 inches between each plant. It likes to be well drained and well watered.

Dill should not be planted near fennel for two reasons. First, cross-pollination takes place, so the following year the plants will be neither true dill nor fennel. Secondly, when you collect the seeds from the drying off plants they are so similar that it will be difficult to tell them apart. The seeds can be gathered and dried easily. The leaves can also be dried.

Fennel *Foeniculum vulgare*, P or A. Fennel is one of

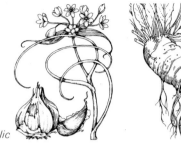

Garlic   Horseradish

the oldest herbs known and might be rated as one of the classics. It is a native of the Mediterranean countries but now grows wild in England along country roadsides.

There are two main varieties, the perennial *Foeniculum vulgare* and the annual *F. vulgare dulce,* known as Florence fennel or Finocchio. The perennial is a graceful sturdy plant, easy to grow to 1.25-1.75 m/4-6 feet. The feathery leaves and seeds are most frequently used commercially.

The annual, Florence fennel, is less robust and grows to about half the height of the perennial. It likes a sunny position with plenty of moisture and, when the base begins to swell, should be earthed up and fed. These solid, white, bulbous looking lower stems do not usually grow as big in England as in France or Italy, where they are very popular as a vegetable, both raw in salads and hors d'oeuvres and cooked cut in slices.

For centuries the leaves have been closely associated with fish, particularly the more oily kinds, presumably to alleviate any digestive difficulties which might be suffered from the richness of the oil.

Both the stem and leaves have a distinct anise flavour, which enhances many sauces and meat dishes as well as fish. In fact fennel and dill are interchangeable as to use.

Fronds of fennel, especially the perennial variety, are much appreciated for flower arrangements. It can be grown in a pot or window box if cut down to 20-25 cm/8-10 inches. Both the leaves and the seeds dry well.

Fines Herbes This is a classical mixture of chervil, chives, parsley and tarragon. It is much used in French cooking. The mixture can be made from fresh or dried herbs, and it freezes well.

Garlic *Allium sativum*, A. Garlic is a sister to the onion, shallot, leek and chive but in flavour is stronger, far more pungent and utterly irreplaceable for putting zest into the dullest dish.

It is a bulb made up of many smaller bulbs of varying sizes called 'cloves'. Recipes calling for 'a clove of garlic' mean one of these and not the whole bulb.

Plant them as you would onions, in a rich friable soil, pressing the cloves in to a depth of about 5 cm/

2 inches and about 15 cm/6 inches apart. When the tops are dry, lift them and dry thoroughly, removing the roots. Store wrapped in foil in a dry place.

Garlic is normally used in cooking in such small quantities (and can always be bought from a greengrocer) that it seems to me unnecessary to use space growing it in a small garden.

In some parts of Britain wild garlic grows in profusion, but this is not the same species as bulb garlic and will never form itself into a bulb.

For cooking, it should be stressed that frying garlic for any length of time dissipates the flavour, so if, for example, a recipe calls for frying onion and garlic, fry the onion first and add the chopped garlic only for the last minute or two.

Horseradish *Amoracia rusticana*, P. The perennial horseradish is perhaps not strictly a herb. However, as it is used not as a vegetable but as a seasoning in many dishes, apart from the traditional horseradish sauce with beef, it may be permissible to include it here.

The roots are the part used in cooking, fresh or dried. They look much like parsnips and, like all deep growing roots, they like a friable, well drained soil so that they can push down easily.

Perennial is the correct description. If horseradish likes your soil it will ramp roughshod over anything which grows in its way.

The flavour is very strong, like mustard, and if eaten in too large a mouthful it will cause great discomfort up the nose and out of the eyes! But a little, especially in a sauce, can make the difference between something prosaic and something exciting.

Horseradish is always grated, minced or ground, fresh or dried. But as ever, there is no comparison between the fresh and the dried root.

Hyssop *Hyssopus officinalis*, P. Hyssop is a perennial plant, growing to about 60 cm/2 feet in height, and it thrives best in partial shade. Sow the seeds in April or propagate by root division in spring or autumn.

There are several varieties, but the hardiest and prettiest is the one which has clusters of blue flowers. Both bees and flower arrangers appreciate its various attractions.

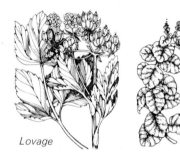

Lovage   Mint

In Europe, the oil is extracted from the plant for use in toilet preparations and the leaves are used in cooking. They have a slightly minty flavour which is said to aid the digestion of fat. The leaves can be dried.

Lovage *Levisticum officinale*, P. Lovage is a hardy perennial which grows to a height of 1.2-1.8 m/4-6 feet. The leaves and flavour are reminiscent of celery, so if there is space it is a valuable component of a herb or kitchen garden for use as a flavouring or vegetable. Use it sparingly, however, because it has a harsher, stronger flavour than celery, and the stems are apt to be a bit stringy.

The great herbalist, John Gerard, wrote of it in his 'Herball' as one of the wonder drugs. It is also said to be a deodorant with a cleansing effect upon the whole system.

The stems can be candied like angelica, but only the very tenderest should be chosen. The leaves can be frozen but do not dry well. The seeds dry well.

Marjoram (Sweet or Knotted) *Origanum marjorana*, A. There are three main kinds of marjoram which are widely used and grown. The sweet or knotted (so called because the flower heads are produced in pairs as greenish clusters when they first appear, looking like knots) is the most useful in cooking and therefore the most useful for cultivation.

Marjoram is a native of the Mediterranean area where it has been known for centuries. In warmer climates it grows as a perennial, but it cannot withstand frost and therefore in colder climates it is treated as an annual. It can be planted in very early spring under glass and then transplanted to the garden in late spring, or planted outdoors in mid-spring. It grows into a bushy plant 30-45 cm/12-18 inches high and has white or pinky-white flowers.

The fresh leaves have an aromatic combination of flavours which is somewhat lost when they are dried. Nevertheless, marjoram is one of the most widely used herbs both by private cooks and food producers. The leaves freeze or dry well.

Pot Marjoram *Origanum onites*, P. Pot marjoram is a perennial and much more robust than sweet marjoram, although it is apt to straggle. It grows to about 60 cm/2 feet and has flat-topped clusters of pinkish-mauve flowers. The roots should be divided in the spring.

The flavour of the leaves in cooking is stronger than that of sweet marjoram, so it should be used with discretion.

Both varieties grow well in window boxes and pots. The leaves should be dried for constant use.
Wild Marjoram *Origanum vulgaris*, P. See Oregano (page 15).

Mint (Spearmint) *Mentha spicata*, P. There are over 20 varieties of mint and many more cross-breeds, but only three or four are normally cultivated.

The most usual type of mint grown commercially for sale fresh from greengrocers and for drying is *M. spicata*, which grows to a height of 60-75 cm/2-2½ feet. It likes a slightly richer soil than most other herbs and ramps like mad, the roots running underground to send up numerous shoots. The best way to contain a plant, to stop it spreading too far, is to plant it in a large pot and sink this into the ground.

Mint propagation is by root division. The plants should be cut back in autumn and, when the fresh shoots appear in the spring, they should be cut from the tough old roots and replanted. This helps to stop 'rust', to which spearmint is rather prone.

It can be grown in a window box, but should be planted in a pot and sunk into the box, so that the roots cannot suffocate any other herb — or grow it in a pot.

Mint is a favourite herb for making herb tea or infusions. The different varieties give their own distinctive flavours. All mint leaves can be frozen or dried.
Bowles Mint *Mentha alopecuroides*, P. This is often called Apple Mint but the name is incorrect. It grows as high or slightly higher than common spearmint and is just as robust, but the flavour of the leaves is stronger and to my mind superior. It is not cut for commercial sale because the leaves wilt quickly when picked. Use it in exactly the same ways as spearmint.
Eau de Cologne Mint *Mentha citrata*, P. This mint is also known as Lemon or Orange Mint. The leaves have a pleasant scent of eau de cologne but taste more of citrus fruit, hence its variety of names.

It is a valuable addition to pot pourri, and is nice hung up in a linen cupboard. It is also good infused

Parsley

in boiling water and sweetened for a hot or cold summer drink.

Pennyroyal *Mentha pulegium*, P. Pennyroyal is another member of the mint family which now grows wild in England. It is the smallest member of the mint family, growing only to 13-15 cm/5-6 inches. The circlets of pretty mauve flowers make it attractive as an edging plant or between paving stones. It has a more pungent flavour than other mints and tastes of peppermint.

Pennyroyal can be grown in window boxes or pots, but the space would be better used for other herbs more often used in cooking. It can be dried.

Peppermint *Mentha piperita*, P. There are two kinds of peppermint—black and white. It is the black variety which is used primarily by the pharmaceutical and confectionary trades, the oil being distilled from the plants. This oil is used to disguise many an unpleasant tasting medicine. It is also the source of all the peppermint flavoured sweets which we enjoy.

Peppermint is cultivated in exactly the same way as spearmint, and grows to about the same height.

Round-leaved or Apple Mint *Mentha suaveolens, M. rotundifolia*, P. As one of its names implies, the leaves are rounded, and with its variegated colours of cream and green it is a most attractive plant which cannot be confused with any other mint.

It is a decorative plant for flower arrangements or in the garden, but is not quite as hardy as the other varieties, as it may die off on heavy soils in very wet weather.

The leaves have a distinct aroma of apple, and the taste is mint with overtones of apple. It is an excellent type with which to make mint sauce, and some consider it the best of all mints for this purpose.

Onion, Ever-ready *Allium cepa perutile*, **Welsh or Ciboule** *A. fistulosum*, **Tree or Egyptian Tree** *A. cepa proliferum*, P. Although these types of onions are not strictly herbs, they all have hollow evergreen leaves which look like a much coarser chive, which I sometimes use chopped in place of chives in the winter. The flavour is definitely inferior, but as a garnish they are a useful substitute.

The Every-ready and Welsh (the name 'Welsh'

comes from a corruption of the German *welsche*, meaning foreign, and has nothing to do with Wales) both have rather elongated small bulbs at the base of cylindrical leaves, which can also be chopped and used as flavouring.

The Tree onion is fascinating and fun to grow as both the leaves and bulbils can be used. This variety has the same type of coarse chive-like leaves, but the flower stems are very large and hollow and a clump of small bulbs, or bulbils, forms on the top of each out of which grow more small green leaves. The stems die off each winter, but the leaves remain green.

The bulbils are more pungent than ordinary onions and can be used for flavouring and pickling. They are good in piccalilli, for example. Propagate and treat in the same way as chives.

Oregano *Origanum vulgare*, P. *O. vulgare* is the wild marjoram which grows both around the shores of the Mediterranean and in many parts of Britain. But there is confusion about the oreganos and marjorams, there being two distinct species of oregano. One grows primarily in Mexico and has a strong, harsh flavour, whereas the oregano used extensively in Italy for pizzas, spaghetti Bolognese and most tomato dishes is the variety we know, both fresh and dried.

The strength of flavour varies considerably according to where the plants grow and the amount of sunshine they enjoy. Even in my herb bed the leaves have a better and stronger flavour during a hot sunny summer than in the cold winter months. It is one of the herbs, together with parsley, chives and thyme, which I regard as indispensable in the kitchen.

It can be grown from seed but is more easily propagated by division in the spring or autumn. I find it withstands the coldest winters, and it is also a splendid plant for window boxes and pots. The leaves freeze and dry well.

Parsley *Petroselinum crispum*, B. There are several kinds of parsley of which the crinkled, curly-leafed type is the best known. It is the most commonly used of all herbs. There is also the Italian, or flat-leafed type (*P. crispum neopolitanum*), which is favoured by Continentals, Greeks and Chinese who consider the flavour superior, but it is not so decorative.

Sage

The turnip-rooted, or Hamburg parsley (*P. crispum tuberosum*) is more of a vegetable than a herb. It has a large tap root like a carrot which can be lifted and stored as other root vegetables. The root tastes of parsley and can be grated or sliced finely as an addition to salads.

Parsley is one of the oldest of all herbs and is known to have been in cultivation for at least 2000 years. It is strictly a biennial, but it is usually treated as an annual because it will not stand a hard frost unless it is protected.

It is slow in germinating and often does not come up at all. There is an old Shropshire saying that 'Parsley must be sown six times, for the devil takes all but the last!' Try at least to get the better of the devil by sowing the seed as follows: make a shallow drill in a well worked moisture-retaining soil and line it with peat; sprinkle in the parsley seeds and cover with about 5 mm/¼ inch of soil. Then be patient for 5-8 weeks before you *may* have to start all over again! Start planting in April or May and then again in August, and keep the soil well watered.

For early parsley, I find that if you plant it in a cold greenhouse or in the house and keep it moist it will germinate well; then it can be transplanted carefully when quite small to a fairly shady position. Parsley does not like being moved when its roots have grown to any depth. It likes a bit of space, 15-20 cm/ 6-8 inches between plants, and above all dislikes too much heat and dryness.

It is an excellent plant for window boxes and pots, especially on a kitchen window sill for handy use all through the winter. Always pick parsley from the outside to allow the young leaves to grow up in the centre; if it is permitted to flower, although the seeds will seed themselves, the plant itself will die.

Parsley freezes well, but I do not recommend drying it.

Rosemary *Rosmarinus officinalis*, P. Rosemary is a native of the Mediterranean areas, particularly Spain and Italy, where the hillsides are covered with these fragrant little bushes which smell heavenly in the heat after a shower of rain.

It is a perennial bush which grows to 1.3 m/4½ feet with attractive pointed evergreen leaves, green on top and grey beneath. It makes a splendid background to any herb or kitchen garden and is well worth growing for its beauty and lovely flavour in cooking.

Rosemary can be propagated by striking cuttings, with a 'heel' if possible, in late summer or autumn (the best time) or at any time in the spring. It is not too hardy and so likes a sunny sheltered spot. A really hard frost may kill it unless it is protected. Do not cut back until it is established, and then only for use or to keep in shape.

The flavour of rosemary gives a delicious fragrance to many dishes, especially lamb, veal and chicken. Try it mixed with other herbs whenever you want a savoury dish to be subtly alluring.

Rosemary can be grown in a tub or pot, but must be pruned carefully to keep the bush compact. The leaves dry well.

Rue *Ruta graveolens*, P. This herb is known as 'stinking rue' from its bitter taste and a smell which many people dislike intensely, although for others it has a peculiar charm.

The perennial shrub came from southern Europe and grows wild along the roadsides in Italy. It is not so much used now; however, in Elizabethan times it was used as a hedge around small formal gardens, for it can stand being well clipped and has attractive blue-green lacy leaves. The yellow flowers are also pretty and continue all through the summer. It is an excellent plant for flower arrangements.

Rue grows to 60 cm/2 feet high and can be planted by seed in a shallow drill or propagated by cuttings — both in the spring. Also in the spring, the established plants should be cut back to 20-30 cm/ 8-12 inches. The leaves can be dried.

Sage *Salvia officinalis*, P. There are several varieties of sage, but the broad-leafed garden type is best for the kitchen. Sage came originally from the Mediterranean area and has been cultivated since the earliest days of recorded history. The name *Salvia* is derived from the Latin word *salvere* — to save or heal. There is an old Arab proverb which has spread to many countries around the world: 'How can a man die if he has sage in his garden?'

Sage is a perennial bush which grows normally to about 60 cm/2 feet, but will grow higher if it can be planted in a sunny, well drained and sheltered position. It is best to replace the bushes every three

Southernwood　　　　　　*Sweet Cicely*

or four years as they become leggy and woody.

It is easy to propagate by cuttings struck in late spring. The flower stalks should be cut off after flowering to encourage the bush to grow in a sturdy compact shape. Sage can be grown in window boxes if carefully pruned, but is better grown in pots.

The leaves can be dried with ease and success, if care is taken to do this at the right time and in the right way. According to old writings, sage is best and at its most beneficial in the spring before it begins to flower and therefore should be picked for drying at this time. The leaves also freeze well.

Savory (Summer) *Satureia hortensis*, A. There are two savories — summer and winter. The summer savory is an annual, growing to about 30 cm/12 inches, whilst the winter savory is a perennial growing to about the same height or a little taller.

Both are natives of the Mediterranean area where they are used extensively in cooking, particularly with beans of all kinds.

The flavour of summer savory is lighter, and almost more feminine, than that of the harder more pungent masculine winter savory. However, both are strong, with a peppery tang which can drown rather than draw out the flavour of a dish, so they should be used with care. It is a good herb also for those on a salt-free diet, as it can alleviate the flat taste of unseasoned food.

Sow seeds of summer savory in shallow, well drained soil in the spring. It can be grown in pots indoors and its fresh leaves can be enjoyed throughout the winter. This is the savory most used commercially for drying.

Savory (Winter) *Satureia montana*, P. A hardy perennial plant which nevertheless should be divided every third year, using the outside shoots and discarding the tough centre.

The leaves can be chopped and mixed with other herbs for freezing, and they can be dried, but are not as satisfactory this way as the summer variety.

Sorrel (French) *Rumex scutatus*, **Common or Garden** *R. acetosa*, P. There are three distinct varieties of sorrel. Two are cultivated and the third is the wild wood sorrel (*Oxalis acetosella*).

Sorrel is one of the few herbs which prefers a rich moist soil and can be grown in the shade. Both varieties are hardy perennials; the garden variety is a larger plant growing to over 60 cm/2 feet. Both should be dug up in early spring every four or five years and divided.

Perhaps the French variety is better for culinary purposes, as the leaves have more flavour than the larger garden one. It should be planted at least 30 cm/12 inches apart.

Sorrel has a slightly bitter flavour and is excellent when mixed with spinach, lettuce or cabbage. The French use it as a vegetable mixed with any of the above in the same way the English use spinach, or as in sorrel soup. Sorrel leaves make a very pleasant addition to lettuce salads or chopped into egg and fish dishes. The leaves can be dried, but I would not recommend this.

Southernwood (Old Man, Lad's Love) *Artemisia abrotanum*, P. Southernwood is another of the old-fashioned herbs, grown now more for its sweet scent than for its use in cooking, as it has a bitter taste.

It is a hardy perennial growing in height to about 1 m/3$\frac{1}{2}$ feet, but it can be clipped to make a neat hedge or rounded bush. For a hedge, the bushes should be planted 30 cm/12 inches apart. Cuttings, struck in autumn or early spring, root easily and thrive in any soil. It is not an evergreen as the leaves, somewhat resembling rosemary, fall in the winter.

This herb derives its delightful name 'Old Man' from a reputation it once had of encouraging hair to grow on balding pates and on the downy chins of young men! 'Lad's Love' came from the custom of a young lover including a sprig in a bouquet for his lass.

Sweet Cicely (Great Chervil, Cow Chervil, Sweet Fern) *Myrrhis odorata*, P. Sweet Cicely is a plant which goes far back in European and Middle Eastern history, even to biblical times. Now it also grows wild in Britain.

It is a perennial growing to a height of 90 cm/3 feet or more and has deeply divided leaves, which make it another plant good for flower decoration. It seeds itself freely, so the flower heads should be cut off before they dry or the seedlings may become a nuisance. The roots can also be divided in spring or autumn. It prefers partial shade and a damp soil.

Tarragon

Thyme

Sweet Cicely has a sweetish flavour faintly reminiscent of anise, but this almost completely disappears during cooking, leaving only the sweetness. For this reason it is a useful herb for those who can eat only small quantities of sugar, or none at all. I find that in stewing such tart fruits as rhubarb and gooseberries, I can cut down the sugar by about half.

To stew fruit this way I lay sprigs of the herb in the bottom of a dish, with more on top of the fruit (mixed with only half the quantity of sugar syrup as usual). Stew gently in the oven, removing the herb before serving. It can also be chopped and mixed with the fruit if preferred.

The leaves and crushed seeds can both be used fairly lavishly for flavouring, and the tap root can be boiled and sliced for use in salads. Sweet Cicely has always been known as an excellent synergic when blended with other herbs. In fact, it is the one herb which seems to bring out the flavour of any other herb with which it is mixed. The leaves can be frozen but do not dry well. The seeds can be dried.

Tarragon Artemisia draconculus, P. It is important to grow the correct variety because the alternative is the Russian (A. dracunculoides) which, although similar in appearance and much more robust, is vastly different in flavour, in fact it has so little that it is not worth growing. Tarragon should be cut down in winter and, as frost can kill it, it should have some protection in any exposed location. It grows up to about 90 cm/3 feet. In temperate climates the French variety never forms a seed, so if any plant has a seed it is the wrong tarragon! Neither does it grow from seed, so it is necessary to start with a plant in the spring or to cadge a root from a friend, for it creeps and sends up numerous shoots.

It is temperamental as to its choice of site and, if it does not get the soil it likes, it simply refuses to grow. I tried to grow it four times, but the soil in the first three attempts was either too rich or too moist. The fourth time I dug good holes 60 cm/2 feet apart, filled them with poor sandy soil and my tarragon grew and grew!

Tarragon vinegar is the way this herb is best known in some countries, but it is also an essential ingredient of many famous sauces and of innumerable other dishes both cooked and uncooked.

It is an excellent herb for growing in a window box or pot (but be careful of the creeping roots). Grown indoors it can be used right through the winter. The leaves can be frozen or dried.

Thyme Thymus vulgaris, P. There are at least 50 varieties of thyme, all attractive in growth, aromatic in perfume and beautiful in flower. It is a native of stony places along the coasts of the Mediterranean but has been cultivated for centuries in most civilised countries. In earlier times its function was more as a relief to the spirit than a pleasure to the stomach.

All thymes are low growing, usually no higher than 23-30 cm/9-12 inches, but some are more miniature than others. The original wild thyme (T. serpyllum) is one of the smallest varieties. It forms a dense mat with bright pink flowers in the summer and a gorgeously sweet scent which is especially strong when crushed.

The variety most used for culinary matters is the Garden or Common thyme (T. vulgaris), which grows as an evergreen in small shrublet form. It can be grown from seed or from a small branch with a piece of root attached, or it can be layered, preferably in early spring. The bushes should be divided every two or three years because they are prone to become leggy and die back in patches. Cut back the bushes after flowering for compact growth, or before flowering if they are required only for cooking.

Thyme is one of the most widely used of all herbs in cooking, being an essential component of a bouquet garni apart from its use in countless savoury dishes. Where it grows and the season of the year when it is picked make a big difference to its flavour.

Caraway Thyme Thymus herba-barona, P. As its name implies, this variety has the unmistakable scent and taste of caraway overlaying the typical thyme flavour.

Lemon Thyme Thymus citriodorus, P. Again the name is descriptive of the flavour, which has a strong overtone of lemon and is less pungent than the common variety. It is one of the two varieties most commonly used in cooking.

All thymes are excellent for growing in a window box or pot, and they are some of the most rewarding herbs for drying.

Growing Herbs in Pots, Window Boxes and Kitchen Gardens

The thought of herb growing might be a trifle daunting to some, but once tried it is apt to become an almost compulsive hobby. There is something very satisfying about growing plants which have so many features. Herbs are not only for show like most plants. They may not look as dramatic as a Jersey Lily, but who can resist the heavenly blue of the borage flower or a pinky-mauve carpet of thyme? Add the soul-soothing pleasure of their scent on a balmy evening (or when the wind blows their perfume into a room or kitchen) to the exquisite satisfaction from their subtle intrusion in any dish, and the fascination of growing herbs can perhaps be comprehended.

Many herbs can occupy a small place. Or a small space can happily be occupied by herbs. Let us start from the beginning.

If a bedsitter- or flat-dweller hankers after the joy of fresh herbs, the answer may be to have two or three pots by a window or on a sill, a window box easily tended from a window, or pots on a roof garden.

Which herbs to grow in them? This must depend upon the taste of the individual. Do you crave the light onion flavour of chives or would you prefer an all-round lifter such as basil or marjoram? Are you an avid 'mint-saucer' with lamb or would you like fennel with your fish and chicken?

I can only suggest my own favourites: parsley, chives, thyme, marjoram or oregano, winter savory, tarragon, mint, fennel, chervil, sage and ever-ready onion. From these each person must select for their own requirements and available space.

Note: In some Australian states, fennel, pennyroyal and sorrel are listed as noxious weeds and permission must be obtained to plant them.

Suggestions for Pots and Window Boxes

Keep the pots as near to the light and sunshine as convenient, putting them out into the rain periodically. The number of herbs in each window box must, of course, depend upon the size of the box and its location, but always allow plenty of room for the roots to spread. There are a few herbs whose roots are so rampant they will grow all over the others in a box and smother them. In these cases, plant each in a pot and then place in the windox box.

Window boxes need not sit upon a window ledge or a balcony. They can also adorn a roof garden, however small, and can be hung on a garage, garden or house wall to brighten and lend interest to an otherwise dull expanse.

The boxes themselves can be made of wood, a composite material or concrete. Pots can be placed in graceful wrought-iron containers standing on legs to form a feature in any room.

They can be made of the ordinary terracotta clay or glazed and decorated pottery for a featured position. Square pots, made in concrete, can be very effective placed outside a kitchen door, on a roof garden or along the edge of any small terrace.

There is also another type of pot which can be both decorative and useful for herb growing. It is called a 'strawberry pot' and has a number of pockets all around it. These pots are ideal for a balcony, roof garden or just outside a kitchen door. To arrange them, plant the most decorative herb, or the one you wish to use most, at the top.

There are now firms selling composition window boxes complete with herb plants. Some of these window boxes include chives, pot marjoram, thyme, sage and tarragon.

Concrete containers have the advantage of lasting longer than their better-known wooden counterparts, especially in the open, and need no upkeep in painting or varnishing. They are also reasonably simple to make at home.

Hints for planting

Cover the hole in the container with some broken bits of crockery, but not so tightly that the water cannot seep through. Then fill with soil.

The best soils to use are those proprietary brands which are especially blended for this type of plant. John Innes Compost No. 3, Levington Compost and EFF Compost are three of the most suitable ones sold in England.

Watering is important. Once a day is sufficient, with only enough to allow the water to seep through to the bottom. The plants should never stand in water.

Plant the herbs about 5-7.5 cm/2-3 inches deep

and press the soil around them firmly. Give them a good watering as soon as they are planted.

Some of the taller growing herbs such as fennel and tarragon become naturally dwarfed by the confined root space. They can also be kept in check by light pruning to make them more compact.

Suggestions for small herb gardens

The variety of shapes and sizes of small gardens is infinite; much must depend upon the space available. There are, however, several points to remember, the most important being that — as already mentioned, but necessary to stress — herbs should be grown as close to the kitchen door as possible.

The ideal herb garden for a cook is one which has a paving from the door to the garden and where the beds are surrounded by paving made from stone, brick or concrete.

Whether the beds are laid out square, round, oblong or hexagonal depends upon the location and number of herbs required. But remember, if you start with four you will soon wish you had room for eight!

Here is another good idea for a small herb garden: build up instead of out. For example, an ideal location would be across the corner of a wall or hedge (but not in a shaded corner), or against a bare kitchen wall. In this case, make sure that only the concrete and not the soil touches the wall, so that the wall cannot absorb any damp. Three tiers built up pyramid fashion make a good and attractive 'garden', allowing a variety of herbs to be tended easily.

Suggestions for large herb gardens

A herb border is a popular method of growing herbs in a kitchen garden. I would suggest that anybody who can should go and see the model herb border at the Royal Horticultural Society Garden at Wisley, near Woking in Surrey, or visit any local herb specialists. When planting a lot of herbs, it helps tremendously to have seen the actual plants growing. Some need much more room for bushing out than others, apart from the different heights to which they grow.

To take but a few examples — rosemary needs to be spaced at least 1 m/3 feet apart, whilst fennel needs 30-45 cm/12-18 inches. Marjoram and mint need 30 cm/12 inches, whereas chives and summer savory need only 15 cm/6 inches.

Herb borders are very attractive planted against a hedge. A herb itself, such as rue or southernwood, may be grown as a hedge, but the aspect must be considered; most herbs need sunshine and light.

The number of plants of each variety must depend upon the size of the family and their taste in food, but be sure to have at least one plant of each of many varieties, so as to try the different fresh flavours.

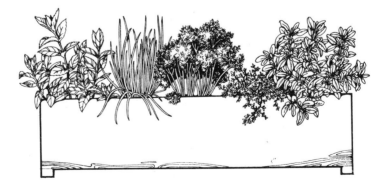

Herb Lawns

The growing of herb lawns, camomile (chamomile) especially, has become very popular in recent years. Here are a few suggestions on what to grow and how to treat them.

Camomile *Anthemis nobilis*. This variety of camomile makes an excellent lawn which is hardy enough to keep green even in hot weather. It is also hardy enough to withstand as much wear and tear from walking as an ordinary lawn. Probably few visitors to Buckingham Palace royal garden parties realise that stretches of one of the lawns there are planted with this camomile. It thrives on light sandy soil, but will grow on anything except clay.

Seeds are sown in the spring in boxes or special seed beds and the plants transplanted to the lawn site as soon as they are large enough to handle, or plants can be bought and planted direct in spring or autumn. They should be planted about 10 cm/4 inches apart.

If a thick sward is desired, the lawn should be mowed *regularly* to prevent flowering. The plants should first be 'topped' when they reach 7.5 cm/3 inches. Then the mower should gradually be lowered to about 1 cm/½ inch. The lawn should be weeded and watered until it has become a really thick mat.

Thyme *Thymus serpyllum*. This is the smallest and hardiest of the thymes and makes a fragrant carpet rather than a strong lawn to walk on. It will not bear much traffic but smells glorious when trodden upon and crushed. It is really more suitable for growing in a special corner or around a garden seat. This variety of thyme is also well suited for planting between paving stones or to make an entire pathway.

It is best planted as established roots in the spring. Keep well watered and weeded as it takes a little time to settle.

It would be a pity to mow a thyme lawn and so forego the beauty of the bright pinky-mauve flowers, but it can be mowed if required.

Pennyroyal *Mentha requieni*. This is one of the smallest of the mint family and, like thyme, is not really hardy enough to bear much traffic. Treat it in the same way as thyme (above).

Storing Herbs

Drying herbs

There is absolutely no comparison between the flavour of fresh and dried herbs, but there are some herbs such as bay leaves, rosemary, thyme, tarragon, etc. which are perfectly satisfactory dried at home. In any case, if they are growing in a garden it would be a pity not to take advantage of them.

Whether dried at home or bought commercially, herbs lose their potency, aroma and flavour if kept for too long. So for home drying do not keep one year's herbs after the next year's supply is ready, or if bought commercially buy little and often.

For storing it is essential to keep bottles *away* from the light. A dark, dry cupboard or drawer is ideal. Here are a few points to remember:

1. Keep each herb separate, without any possibility of one becoming mixed with another.
2. Have the storage bottles or jars clean and clearly marked before the herbs are dry and ready for packaging.
3. Do not keep dried herbs in a moist atmosphere, even in airtight containers.

For drying leaves, the best time to pick them is as soon as the flower buds appear on the plant but before they begin to open. At this period, the greatest abundance of natural oils is concentrated in the leaves, which will give the fullest flavour when dried.

Small-leaved herbs, such as thyme, savory and tarragon, can be picked by the branch and hung up to dry in bundles. Large-leaved ones, such as mint, sage and basil, are better picked separately from the growing branches. Be sure that each leaf is perfect without spot or blemish. Pick them in warm dry weather in the morning, after the dew has evaporated and before the sun has become hot enough to draw out the natural oils.

Place those tied in bundles in a warm dry place such as an airing cupboard where they can be hung from slatted shelves and left only until they are dry (brittle) enough to bottle. This should not take more than a few days. A kitchen or bathroom, although warm, is not good because of the steam which occurs in both. If they have to be left in a passage, garage or other location which may be dusty, tie them in a piece of muslin.

The best temperature for the first twenty-four hours is about 32°C/90°F; then it can come down to 21-26°C/70-80°F. Unless the weather is persistently wet and the herbs have had to be picked in a moist condition, it is not advisable to dry them in an oven. If this is necessary, the temperature should be kept as low as possible. Neither is it good to dry them

in the sun. A dark place allows them to retain their colour.

When the leaves are dry, strip them off the branches and store in airtight bottles or jars, or rub through a wire sieve.

For the larger leaves, place on a tray covered with absorbent kitchen paper and dry them at the same temperature. Keep turning them over and around so that they dry evenly. When they are brittle enough, crush into small pieces before turning into airtight containers, or rub through a wire sieve.

Seeds of herbs for drying should be allowed to dry partially on the stems before collection. Then strip them off and place on paper-covered trays to dry. Keep moving them around so that they dry evenly.

Freezing herbs

Herbs freeze surprisingly well, but the small rather hard-leaved varieties such as thyme, rosemary and savory which dry so well are, I consider, only worth freezer space either chopped and mixed with other herbs or in packets as bouquet garni.

There are several ways of freezing herbs. My favourite is to chop them when clean and dry with a sharp knife (or pair of scissors for chives); do not use a mincing machine of any kind, as this tears the leaves. Then pack them into tiny plastic boxes with their own lids (those which come with individual servings of butter or jam in some restaurants are ideal), or use any really small bottle or plastic container with a lid. One, two or three can then be used as required. I also like to freeze mixed herbs in the same way to give a fresh flavour to an assortment of dishes throughout the winter.

Packets of bouquet garni can be tied together, leaving a long piece of string dangling from each. Open freeze (laying each one flat) separately, and when frozen place a piece of film between them before wrapping them all in polythene or foil for storage. Each bouquet can thus be removed individually as required.

Another method which is often advocated is to chop the herbs and pack them into ice cube trays with water. When frozen, the cubes can be removed and tied in a plastic bag for storage. But I find this leaves the herb, especially parsley, too wet for garnishing, and the extra liquid when the ice melts will dilute a sauce.

A third method is to freeze sprigs of herbs, then as *soon* as they are removed from the freezer they can be crunched up in the hand to eliminate chopping.

A last heartfelt plea – DO please mark every packet or bottle at once, so that there can never be any mistake.

Spices and Where They Grow

Allspice (Pimento, Jamaica Pimento, Jamaica Pepper, Clove Pepper) *Pimenta officinalis.* The allspice tree grows in the Caribbean islands and Central America and, although the tree will grow in other parts of the world, it will not bear fruit anywhere else.

The evergreen tree grows 7.5-9 m/25-30 feet in height. The fruit is harvested when mature but still green. After drying, the berry is dark reddish-brown, round, with a roughish surface and about the size of a pea.

The name allspice comes from the aroma and flavour of the seeds which resemble a combination of cinnamon, cloves and nutmeg. But it should not be confused with 'mixed pickling spice' which is a mixture of allspice berries and many other spices.

Note: Pimento should not be confused with pimiento (with an extra i), which is a species of capsicum (green and red sweet peppers).

Anise *Pimpinella anisum.* The seeds we use come from an annual herbaceous plant growing to about 30 cm/12 inches high. Originally coming from the region east of the Mediterranean, the plants now grow also in Spain, Turkey, Bulgaria, Syria and the United States.

Anise fruit, commonly called aniseed, is tiny, brown and oval, with an unmistakable flavour of liquorice. It is from this that such liqueurs as anisette are made.

Capsicum. Capsicum is a species of herbaceous plant, annual and perennial, of which there are many varieties. Capsicums cover a variety of fruit we know by other names. For example, chillies (*C. frutescens* and others) are the smallest of the capsicum family, which we know as frantically hot. In tropical climates they are grown and used fresh, particularly in curries. In Europe and temperate climates they are used dried or ground as chilli powder, red pepper or cayenne, of which cayenne is traditionally the hottest. This may be orangey-red, whereas chilli powder and red pepper are usually a brighter red. Chillies are also sold in flakes as 'crushed red pepper'.

Paprika comes from another species, *C. annuum.* Although much the same colour as cayenne and chilli powder, it is nothing like as hot.

In Europe there are many types of paprika, but in England and the United States the usual kind is the 'sweet' type, which is a brilliant red colour and invaluable for garnishing many a dull-coloured dish. Spanish cuisine also uses this type exclusively.

Then there are sweet pepper flakes which are now sold dried for use in stews. They are the dried flesh of the much larger red and green capsicums, which we know as 'sweet peppers'.

Caraway *Carum carvia.* Caraway is a biennial plant, reaching a height of about 60 cm/2 feet. The seeds, which are used in cooking, have a tendency to shatter when ripe, so they have to be harvested at night or before the dew has dried off them.

Caraway grows happily in northern Europe, particularly Holland. The seeds are larger than anise seeds, but otherwise look much like them. They also have a similar, though stronger, flavour of liquorice. The German name for caraway is 'Kümmel', and the oil from caraway goes into making the famous liqueur of that name.

It is now possible to buy ground caraway seeds, but grinding seems to minimise the strength of the liquorice flavour. The unusual spicy flavour is delicious in a green bean salad and with courgettes, cabbage, tomatoes and many other vegetables.

Cardamom *Elettaria cardamomum.* The perennial bush cardamom plant grows from 1.75-3.5 m/6-12 feet high. It is a native of India but is now grown commercially in India, Sri Lanka and Guatemala. It is the second most expensive spice in the world (the first is saffron), because each seed pod has to be snipped off the plant by hand with a pair of scissors.

The dried and bleached pods are buff coloured, three sided and 5 mm-1 cm/$\frac{1}{4}$-$\frac{1}{2}$ inch long. Inside are numerous small black seeds which have a delightfully warm, slightly pungent and highly aromatic flavour. The Vikings discovered cardamom on their travels a thousand or more years ago, and took it back to Scandinavia. To this day, true Danish pasties always have a faint aroma of cardamom.

Cayenne *Capsicum frutescens.* See Capsicum (above).

Chilli *Capsicum frutescens.* See Capsicum (page 28).

Cinnamon *Cinnamomum zeylanicum, C. cassia.* The evergreen cinnamon tree is a member of the laurel family and a native of the Far East. The pungent sweet flavour which we know as cinnamon comes from the dried bark of the tree. This is stripped off and, after going through several processes, emerges dried and curled into what are known as 'quills' or 'pipes'. These are the sticks of cinnamon which we buy. Cinnamon is also sold in powder form.

The spice which comes from Sri Lanka is slightly different in flavour from that which is grown in Indonesia and Vietnam. It is from Indonesia that America imports its cinnamon spice, as the flavour of this variety is preferred there.

The flavour of cinnamon and the scent from it are used in great quantity world-wide. It is one of the essential components of many mixtures of spices, both sweet and savoury.

Cloves *Eugenia aromatica.* The clove tree is a beautiful evergreen which grows to a height of 12 m/40 feet. It is a native of the Moluccas or Spice Islands, but is now grown commercially in Tanzania, most of the West Indian islands, Indonesia, the Malagasy Republic and in other places with tropical climates.

It is said that nutmegs have to smell the sea and the clove has to see it. From early accounts the unspoiled islands were a beautiful sight, with deep green trees covered with tiny brilliant red flowers. The fragrance which wafted out to the ships told the sailors that they had arrived at the 'Garden of Spices' — the Moluccas.

The clove we use is the dried, unopened flower bud, like a little round ball on the end of the stem. As the buds have to be picked at this stage for drying, the beauty and scent of the opened blossoms has to be sacrificed.

The name clove is derived from the Latin word *clavus*, a nail, which the 1 cm/½ inch long dried clove resembles.

It takes 4-7000 dried clove buds to make 0.5 kg/1 lb of spice, so naturally they command a price commensurate with their rarity.

Coriander *Coriandrum sativum.* Coriander is a herb growing to about 60 cm/2 feet, but it is the seed which is used as a spice. The seed should not be picked from the plant until it is ripe, and should then be thoroughly dried, as the green seed has a rather unpleasant taste.

Pliny, in the 1st century AD, wrote that the finest coriander seeds came from Egypt. Today they are still an essential spice for flavouring food in India, China, the Arab world and Mexico. In the United States, Great Britain and Europe the spice is included in sausages of various kinds.

Cumin (Cummin, Comino seed, Jeera) *Cuminum cyminum.* Cumin or jeera is a small annual plant, a native of the Nile Valley but for centuries cultivated in India, Africa, Morocco, China, Malta, Sicily, Palestine, Lebanon, the United States, Latin America and the Mediterranean area.

Cumin seed looks like anise, dill or caraway seed but has a strong aromatic flavour unlike any of them. It is an essential ingredient in curry powder and in American chili powder. It is also used liberally in Near and Middle Eastern and Latin American cooking. The Scandinavians, Dutch and Swiss use it in cheeses, and the Germans use it in pork and sauerkraut dishes.

Curry powder. In India and Sri Lanka curry powder is ground freshly each day by housewives and professional cooks alike from a variety of spices. Each person varies the number and quantity of the spices they use. The flavours and heat are also varied according to the type of food to be curried.

Commercial curry powder is a mixture of anything from 12 to 20 different spices. The heat of each variety varies considerably from relatively mild to extremely hot, according to the amount of ground chillis included.

From specialist shops in Britain and the United States it is also possible to buy garam masala — a mixture of ground spices with less heat than some curry powders — to use when wished or to mix with curry powder if a large range of different spices are not stocked at home.

Fenugreek *Trigonella foenum-graecum.* Fenugreek, also known as 'Greek Hay Seed' or 'Methi' in the East, is an annual growing to a height of about 60 cm/2 feet. It is indigenous to south-eastern Europe but has been grown in India, Egypt, Morocco and Lebanon for centuries.

Fenugreek is a little known spice, yet the ground seeds are one of the essential spices in curry powder. The herb was used in ancient times as a medicine and the whole plant given to cattle as fodder.

Ginger *Zingiber officinale.* Ginger is an herbaceous perennial consisting of an underground stem, or rhizome, from which leafy shoots grow up to 1 m/ 3 feet in height.

A native of India and China, it was one of the first true Oriental spices to make its way westward. Now it is grown in other tropical climates such as West Africa, Jamaica, the West Indies and Central America. The Chinese cuisine uses ginger in all its forms as the most important single flavouring for its incomparable food.

Ginger is sold in many forms, some peeled, some unpeeled. Most countries growing it for export classify it into several grades. It can be bought freshly preserved or 'green', and this is the best flavour for savoury dishes. These pieces of rhizome (root) are found in specialist shops. They look dried, but when peeled are a greeny-cream colour, juicy and very hot. They can be kept wrapped tightly in foil in a refrigerator for many weeks, and in a freezer for many months. Ginger can also be bought in small cans already peeled and labelled 'green ginger'. This is delicious for Chinese dishes of all kinds and is not quite as hot as the fresh root.

Ginger is also sold completely dried and very hard. This type is always an ingredient in pickling spice. It can be softened by soaking in cold water overnight. It is sold ground in powder form, which can be stored indefinitely in an airtight container. Crystallised and preserved ginger are made from fresh roots and are considered confections rather than spices.

Juniper *Juniperus communis.* The juniper tree is a small evergreen which is native to Europe, the Arctic and northern parts of Africa. The berries take two to three years to ripen on the tree; then they are picked and dried. They should be crushed (with the back of a spoon) before use and used with care since they have a strong taste. They make a particularly good flavouring for strong, rich foods such as game, hare, venison and pork.

Juniper berries are popular for smoking some kinds of meat and they also provide the flavouring in the manufacture of gin.

Mace. See Nutmeg (below).

Mustard, Black or Brown *Brassica nigra,* **White or Yellow** *Brassica sinapsis alba.* There are two kinds of mustard grown as spices, commonly known as black or brown and white or yellow. Both are herbaceous annual plants which came originally from Europe and south-east Asia but are now grown extensively for export in Britain, Denmark, Canada and the United States.

Mustard as a spice has been known to man since prehistoric times. It got its name from a corruption of 'must-seeds'. When the Romans occupied Britain they mixed the crushed seeds with 'must' — the newly pressed juice from grapes before fermentation sets in.

Unlike other spices, neither the seeds nor even the crushed powder have a scent. It is only when the enzyme activity is started by the addition of liquid that mustard develops its pungent character. It can be mixed into a paste with water, white wine or vinegar.

Nutmeg and Mace *Myristica fragrans.* The bushy nutmeg tree grows up to 9-12 m/30-40 feet in height and is said to like to 'smell the sea'. At all events it is certainly an island plant, a native of the Moluccas, but it is now cultivated also in Indonesia and on the island of Penang in Malaysia.

The ripe fruit resembles a peach in appearance. In some places it is allowed to fall and is then collected every morning, whilst in others it is collected off the tree by means of a long pronged stick with a basket attached.

The outer husk is removed first, and some of this is preserved in syrup — a delicacy in Indonesia. Then the bright red lacy aril or fruit fibre — the mace — can be seen surrounding the little brown nutmeg.

The mace and nutmeg are both dried slowly. The mace is often ground on the spot and only a small quantity is exported as blades of mace. The nutmeg, on the other hand, is usually exported as a whole nut

Arind Lamb (see page 73); Quick 'n Easy Lamb Curry (see page 63)
Overleaf: Herb and Spice Butters (see page 88)

and is then ground by manufacturers as required for their trade.

Nutmeg and mace were not known in European history before AD 600, and it was not until the Dutch had cornered the spice trade in the Moluccas in the 16th century that these two powerful and wonderful spices became really well known.

Paprika *Capsicum annuum.* See Capsicum (page 28).

Pepper *Piper nigrum.* The pepper plant is a perennial climbing vine which grows wild up trees to a height of 6-7.5 m/20-25 feet, but when cultivated it is kept down to not more than 4.5 m/15 feet.

It is a truly tropical plant, growing only within about ten degrees of the Equator, and is now grown and exported mainly from India, Sri Lanka, Indonesia, Malaysia and Brazil.

The peppercorns we know grow in racemes, like grapes but not so close to each other. As the berries ripen they turn from green to yellow to red. Those destined for sale as black pepper are picked when they are still slightly underripe. As they dry, the colour changes to black and this outer hull is left on. It gives a more pungent flavour than white pepper.

White pepper is the fully ripe berry, soaked soon after picking to soften the outer hull. This can then be rubbed off easily, leaving the smooth parchment-coloured cone with its milder flavour.

Black or white pepper should be used in cooking according to the type and colour of the dish. But there is no substitute for freshly ground black peppercorns from a pepper mill whenever a dish warrants this.

Poppy seeds *Papaver somniferum.* This is the opium poppy, an annual which can grow as high as 1.25 m/4 feet, but usually only to 60 cm-1 m/2-3 feet. The plant came originally from the Mediterranean area but is now widely cultivated. The best seeds, however, come from Holland.

The deep blue-black poppy seeds sold commercially should be genuine blue poppy seeds but are sometimes white ones coloured blue artificially. This dye is water soluble, so a few seeds soaked in water will soon tell you whether they are genuine or not.

Although opium and other narcotics are obtained from this plant, there is no need to worry about the seeds. The seeds cannot form until after the plant has matured to the point where it has lost all of its opium content.

Poppy seeds are scattered over bread of different kinds, mixed with pasta and crushed and mixed with sugar and syrup as fillings for pastries and cakes. A poppy seed grinder is a common gadget in a European kitchen, although it is seldom found in British homes. To crush the seeds without the special grinder, they should be soaked in water for several hours, then crushed between paper or polythene with a rolling pin or bottle. Toasting whole seeds in a heavy frying pan over a gentle heat, or in a moderately hot oven (190°C, 375°F, Gas Mark 5) for 5-7 minutes brings out the flavour.

Saffron *Crocus sativus.* The spice saffron comes from the stigmas of the mauve flowering autumn crocus. Each crocus has only three stigmas which must be picked by hand and it takes 225,000 stigmas to make 450 g/1 lb of spice. This makes it the world's most expensive spice. Fortunately, a little goes a long way.

The saffron crocus is a native of Asia and the Mediterranean area and now is exported chiefly from Spain and Portugal. In both these countries, naturally, it is used extensively in cooking.

The dried stigmas are usually sold in tiny packets. Before use they should be crushed in a pestle and mortar (no Spanish kitchen is without one) and dissolved in water (preferably hot), milk or whatever liquid is being used in the dish.

For certain dishes saffron is indispensable — for example, in the classic French *bouillabaisse* from Marseilles, Spanish *paella* and *arroz con pollo*, and England's Cornish saffron cakes.

Sesame (Benne or Bene seed) *Sesamum indicum.* Sesame is an annual which grows up to 1.25 m/4 feet. The mature pods are apt to burst at a touch, scattering the small white seeds, which makes harvesting by machinery difficult. But so valuable are the seeds for their high protein and mineral oil content that new strains of the plant are being grown to eliminate this hazard.

Countless nations have used it, and still do, as oil: in their medicines, in cosmetics and in their food.

35

Crab and Mushroom Mousse (see page 52)

In the Middle East sesame paste, called 'tahini', is used extensively in cooking. It can be bought in health food stores or at grocers specialising in Greek, Lebanese or Syrian products.

Turmeric *Curcuma longa*. Turmeric is an herbaceous, perennial plant of the ginger family, whose leaves grow to about 60 cm/2 feet high. But like ginger it is the rootstock or rhizome which is used as a spice.

Dried and ground, the spice is bright orange in colour and in cooking can be interchanged with saffron for both colour and flavour.

Turmeric is an essential ingredient of curry powder and, together with cumin seed, I find a bit extra adds that little something to curries. It is also the spice used with mustard in mustard pickles and sauce.

Turmeric grows in so many countries in the Orient, West Indies and South America and is used in such versatile ways for flavouring, perfumery, dyeing and the chemical industry, that it is difficult to know from where or how it actually originated. At all events it is an Oriental spice par excellence, which deserves to be known and used far more widely in the West.

Vanilla *Vanilla planifolia*. Vanilla could be called the 'Queen of Seasonings', coming as it does from rare and beautiful pale yellow orchids. These orchids grow in clusters of a dozen or more blossoms, which usually flower for only one day.

The vanilla vine is a native of tropical America, particularly Mexico, although it is now also cultivated in Madagascar, the Seychelles, Java, Tahiti and other tropical areas.

The fruit, or vanilla bean, is similar in many respects to the familiar string or green bean – but with an exquisite flavour. It makes sweet dishes taste sweeter and coaxes out the flavour of chocolate, coffee and fruit.

When harvested the bean is green in colour and completely odourless and flavourless. It takes up to six months of careful and skillful labour in curing, fermenting and drying to produce the dark brown, nearly black colour and characteristic fragrance. The oil, distilled from the bean and widely used, is called 'vanillin'.

Vanilla essence can be bought in bottles, but in order to enjoy the true flavour of vanilla it is important to buy the pure essence distilled from the bean itself, *not* the synthetic essence. The inimitable flavour of vanilla can best be enjoyed to the full by using the bean, either in an infusion if liquid is called for or as vanilla sugar.

The bean can be rinsed, dried and used many times before the flavour begins to recede; one pod will last at least four to six weeks. For an infusion, the liquid should be brought to the boil and the vanilla bean dropped in as the pan is removed from the heat. Then allow 10-30 minutes' infusion, depending upon the strength of flavour required.

For vanilla sugar, fill a bottle with castor sugar and, depending on the size, push in one or two beans. Or cut one bean in half lengthways – this works faster. Leave the bottle tightly closed for the flavour to permeate the sugar. Remember that vanilla sugar is sweeter than plain sugar, so use carefully.

A–Z of Culinary Uses for Herbs and Spices

In the food industry the difference between herbs, spices and condiments is as follows:

Herbs are classified as soft-stemmed aromatic plants whose herbaceous tops are gathered. They are used fresh or dried, when the leaves are usually rubbed off the hard stalks.

Many of these plants grow wild in temperate climates, especially around the Mediterranean area and in the United States, Mexico and Canada, where they are now also grown commercially in enormous quantities.

Spices are dried aromatic vegetable products, usually only parts of plants such as roots, bark, flower buds, fruits and seeds. They grow in a variety of tropical countries.

Condiments are also spices (aside from salt) and are usually added to food at the table or after cooking.

To these should be added those composite spices and herbs which have been pioneered in America and are now sold in Britain and many other countries. For example, Apple pie spice, a mixture amongst others of cinnamon, nutmeg and sugar; Pumpkin pie spice, a mixture of cinnamon, ginger, nutmeg, cloves, etc.; Meat tenderiser, composed of salt, papain (from papaw fruit), etc.; Barbecue seasoning, a mixture of spices, dextrose, monosodium glutamate and liquid smoke flavour; Italian seasoning, a mixture of six or seven herbs; and countless others.

There are also important composite condiments such as Seasoned salt, a mixture of sixteen or seventeen ingredients such as spices, sugar, monosodium glutamate, onion and herbs mixed with the salt; Seasoned pepper, with sweet peppers, spices, sugar, lactic acid, etc.; Hickory smoked salt; etc.

Monosodium Glutamate is described in the Dictionary of Nutrition and Food Technology as 'Glutamate, Sodium. Sodium salt of the amino acid, glutamic acid. Enhances the flavour of some foods, especially meat and vegetables, apparently by stimulating the taste buds. Commercially manufactured from sugar beet pulp and wheat gluten. Glutamic acid has two acidic groups and it is the monosodium salt, known as MSG, that has this flavour property. First introduced as a flavouring agent under the Japanese name of "Ajinomoto".' Monosodium glutamate has in itself no nutritional value.

General Points to remember for the use of herbs and spices in cooking (see also Storing Herbs, page 26), are:

1. The art of flavouring in cooking is to use *just* sufficient to enhance the subtlety of a dish, not to drown the inherent flavour of the food.

2. Ground spices give out their flavour quickly, so for any long cooking dishes, such as soups and stews, add them only for the last 20-30 minutes.

3. In most cases use at least twice the quantity of fresh as dried herbs to give the same intensity of flavour, although the flavour of the fresh herb far outstrips that of its dried counterpart.

4. Different herbs and spices have an affinity with different types of food. Try the recommended combinations first, then experiment with any others you may fancy.

A survey carried out by one of the world's largest spice houses says, 'Few women know how to use spices and herbs, and therefore fear them. Yet it can be the difference between good and bad cooking.'

The favourite dozen herbs and spices amongst home cooks, according to a survey among cookery editors by one of the largest British food manufacturers, is given as follows: nutmeg, cinnamon, bay leaf, cloves, ginger, marjoram, rosemary, sage, thyme, paprika, mixed spice and tarragon.

Culinary uses for herbs

Angelica Flavour is penetrating but difficult to describe. Be careful in use as many people dislike the flavour. Use *stems* for crystallizing to decorate cakes and sweets; in cakes. Use *leaves* and *root* for stewing with fruit (to give sweetness in place of some sugar); in marmalade; in marinades for fish and shellfish dishes; chopped leaves in salads; in wine cups and fruit drinks.

Balm Pleasant light lemon scent and flavour. Use chopped *leaves* (added towards the end of cooking)

Bergamot   *Borage*

in soups; fish dishes; poultry dishes; sauces; stuffings; mixed with other herbs in salads; marinades; stewed fruit; cold drinks; iced tea. Use whenever a light lemon flavour is desired. Pretty as a garnish.

Basil Slight clove pepper flavour. Use chopped *leaves* in soups; fish and shellfish dishes; egg dishes; meat, game and poultry stews; sausage dishes; salads — particularly potato, rice, bean and beetroot; vegetables — particularly courgettes, aubergines, beetroot and onions; all tomato dishes; sauces — especially for pasta (such as Pesto) with garlic. Use *ground* in French dressing.

Bay Flavour is strong and spicy. Use *leaves* from the beginning of cooking in soups; fish dishes; meat stews; with boiled beef, gammon, pickled pork, tongue, poultry; in marinades; sauces; milk puddings and custards (remove when flavour is strong enough). Essential component of bouquet garni.

Bergamot Light lemon flavour. Use *leaves* and *flowers* with salads; white wine cups, tisanes; as garnishes (especially the flowers).

Bog Myrtle Strong, aromatic, rather bitter flavour. Use *leaves* (chopped) and *berries* (crushed) in meat and poultry stews.

Borage Light cucumber flavour. Use young *leaves* with fish; salads — especially potato and cucumber; cottage cheese. Use *flowers* to float on fruit salads; sprays of leaves and flowers to garnish cold drinks; claret cup; Pimms. Flowers can be crystallised.

Bouquet Garni The classic bouquet garni is composed of a small bay leaf, three or four sprays of parsley including the stalks, and a sprig of thyme — all tied in muslin for easy extraction before serving. To these may be added any other herb which is desired for any particular dish.

Burnet Flavour resembles cucumber. Use *leaves* in salads; cream and cottage cheese; with tarragon and rosemary in stews and sauces; in spiced vinegars.

Chervil Slight anise flavour. Use *leaves* (always at the end or after cooking) in soups; fish dishes; salads; omelette and egg dishes; sauces — particularly Béarnaise, Remoulade, Gribiche, Ravigote; herb butters; cheese dishes. Mixes well with other herbs and is an essential herb for the French 'fines herbes'. Pretty as a garnish.

Chives Mild onion flavour. Use scissor-snipped *leaves* in soups; fish dishes; salads of all kinds; vegetables of all kinds, but especially mashed and baked potatoes; omelettes and egg dishes; sauces; cream and cottage cheese. Irreplaceable as a garnish, for topping light coloured dishes particularly. Mixes well with chopped parsley and chervil. Use *flowers* to garnish soup and savoury dishes.

Coriander Leaves and green seeds have an unpleasant smell (see page 29). Use young chopped *leaves* in soups; beef stews and puddings; salads. Use *leaves* and green *seeds* in curries, particularly the southern Indian varieties.

Costmary Slight minty flavour and somewhat bitter. Use chopped *leaves* (sparingly) in soups; stews; tisanes; for brewing ale. Is best mixed with other herbs.

Dill Slight anise flavour. Use chopped *leaves* (added at the end of cooking) in soups; fish dishes; salads; vegetable dishes — particularly marrow, tomatoes, beetroot, cabbage, cucumber, mushrooms; sauces — particularly for fish; egg dishes; pickling cucumber. Use *sprigs* and leaves as a garnish for fish dishes; cucumber; cheese; open sandwiches. Use *seeds* in fish dishes; grilled lamb and pork; stews; sauerkraut, cabbage, and cauliflower; cheese dishes.

Fennel Stronger anise flavour than dill. Similar to dill in every respect, but even better for fish, particularly oily fish. Grill fish over *sprigs* of dried fennel, otherwise use in exactly the same way as dill. Use *seeds* for a fish court bouillon.

Fines Herbes The classical mixture of four herbs — chervil, chives, parsley and tarragon. Can be made from fresh (much better) or dried herbs. Mix in equal

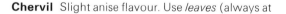

Fennel

Mint

quantities. Use with fish; poultry; in omelettes and egg dishes; salads; vegetables; sauces.

Garlic More pungent than onion. For chopping and crushing do not use a wooden board unless kept solely for garlic. Use in soups; fish dishes; roast lamb; meat stews; poultry dishes; beefburgers; pasta dishes; canned baked and butter beans; vegetable dishes — particularly tomatoes, green peppers, artichokes, aubergine, spinach; salads of all kinds; sauces; French dressing; cheese dishes; marinades; garlic bread; garlic and mixed herb butters.

Horseradish Very strong, hot, pungent flavour like mustard. Use *roots* grated, minced, or ground as a sauce (made with cream and/or vinegar) with shellfish; smoked fish — especially sturgeon and eel; roast beef, salt beef and other beef dishes; tongue; poultry dishes; beetroot and tomatoes.

Hyssop Slightly bitter, minty flavour. Use *leaves* and tender *tops* in soups; with oily fish such as eel; in stews; salads; stuffings; fruit cocktails, particularly cranberry; fruit pies; tisanes;

Lovage Flavour like celery but stronger and harsher. Use *stems* (but only young ones) as celery; candy them as angelica. Use *leaves* and *seeds* in place of celery for soups; stews; salads. Use in any dish to replace celery, but use sparingly.

Marjoram Sweet, spicy flavour. Very versatile in cooking. Use chopped *leaves* (towards the end of cooking) in soups; meat dishes; poultry dishes; vegetables — particularly potatoes, carrots, cabbage, celery, green beans; salads; egg dishes; fish and meat sauces; cheese dishes.

Mint Strong spearmint flavour. Use chopped *leaves* for grilling lamb and veal chops; vegetables — particularly carrots, aubergine; dried beans; with vinegar as sauce for lamb; mint jelly; stuffings; tisanes. Use *sprigs* for boiling potatoes, peas.
Bowles Mint Flavour superior to spearmint in my opinion. Use in exactly the same manner.
Peppermint Strong flavour of peppermint. Use *leaves* in salads; jellies, fruit cups; sweets and candies.

Round-leaved or Apple Mint Distinct flavour of apples overlaying the mint. Said by some to be superior to other mints for mint sauce. Use *leaves* as garnish for salads; in fruit salads; fruit cups; tisanes.

Onion, Ever-ready or Welsh Use scissor-snipped *leaves* in place of chives in winter, but flavour is weaker. Use small *bulbs* when only a little flavouring of onion is required.

Onion Tree Use *leaves* in place of chives as above. Use *bulbils*, which have a stronger flavour than onion, for pickling; in piccalilli; or in small quantities for flavouring any dish.

Oregano Stronger and more pungent than marjoram. Use chopped *leaves* with pasta and most Italian dishes, particularly spaghetti Bolognese and pizzas; meat stews; chilli con carne; rabbit, veal and poultry dishes; stuffings; tomato sauces.

Parsley Our most versatile herb with its own distinctive flavour. *Stalks* have a stronger flavour than leaves, so use in stews; stocks; marinades. Use whole *sprigs* for bouquet garni and as stalks. Use chopped *leaves* in soups; fish dishes; egg dishes; meat and poultry dishes; with ham; tongue; veal; salads; vegetables; sauces, especially for broad beans; Maître d'hôtel butter, herb butters; mixed with other herbs for any dish; as a garnish for any savoury dish which needs colour.

Pennyroyal Peppermint flavour but more pungent than other mints. Use *leaves* chopped as garnish for tea and other beverages in place of mint.

Rosemary Strong distinctive flavour which is apt to overpower other herbs if used in quantity. Use *sprigs* under roast lamb, veal or placed inside a roasting chicken; in pot roasts; marinades. Use *leaves* chopped in soups; fish dishes; with veal; tripe; bacon and ham; any meat or game stew; in poultry or rabbit dishes; vegetable dishes — particularly marrow, peas, sweet peppers, potatoes; stuffings; bread and scones mixed with other herbs.

Rue Rather bitter flavour. Use *leaves* sparingly in salads; salad sandwiches; cream cheese.

Savory Winter

Sage Strong distinctive flavour, very slightly bitter, which goes well with fatty foods. Use chopped *leaves* for pea soup; with pork; goose; duck; sausages; in meat stews; meat loaves; salads; with vegetables — particularly tomatoes, sweet peppers, aubergine, onions; dried beans; in stuffings; sauces with other herbs; herb bread and pastry with other herbs; tisanes. Use leaves whole for Saltimbocca alla Romana (Italian veal dish with ham).

Savory Summer savory has a more delicate flavour than the perennial winter variety. Both have a peppery taste (the winter variety is quite strong), so use with care. A good herb for mixing with others. Use *sprigs* for boiling with broad beans and all kinds of green beans; in marinades. Use chopped *leaves* in soups; over fish; with other herbs in egg dishes; beef dishes; with game; poultry; veal; pork; in sauces; with vegetables, either alone or mixed with other herbs, such as broad beans, green beans, carrots, tomatoes, beetroot, cauliflower and others; in shortcrust pastry for meat and vegetable pies; with other herbs for bread.

Sorrel Rather bitter, acid flavour. *Leaves* used for salad with lettuce; as a vegetable mixed with spinach and/or lettuce; as a soup mixed with spinach, lettuce, or cabbage; mixed with cream, white, or Béchamel sauce for pork or fatty birds.

Southernwood Rather bitter flavour. Use young *leaves* chopped in salads; sparingly in cakes.

Sweet Cicely Sweetish flavour faintly resembling anise. Good herb for mixing with others. Use *sprigs* for stewing tart fruits such as rhubarb, gooseberries, currants, plums and damsons. Use chopped fresh *leaves* in soups; salads; with root vegetables.

Tarragon Liquorice and slightly bitter flavour; a prince of herbs. Use chopped *leaves* in dishes with eggs; chicken; kidneys; sweetbreads; in tarragon butter for fish and shellfish dishes; with vegetables — particularly mushrooms, courgettes, artichokes, tomatoes, beetroot, cabbage; in salads; as 'fines herbes'; in sauces such as Béarnaise, Tartare, Ravigote, Verte; stuffings.

Thyme Common thyme has a distinctive strong flavour. Lemon and caraway thymes are less strong, with additional flavours as their names imply. One of the most versatile culinary herbs. Use *sprigs* for bouquet garni; stock; marinades. Use chopped *leaves* in soups; fish and shellfish dishes (particularly lemon thyme); meat and poultry dishes of every kind; with other herbs; in meat loaves; with game such as hare, pigeon, venison; stuffings for all fish and meat; egg dishes; sauces; salads; with vegetables — particularly beetroot, aubergine, onions, carrots, tomatoes, beans, mushrooms; with pasta and rice dishes; in bread and pastry mixed with other herbs.

Culinary uses for spices

Allspice Flavour resembles a mixture of cinnamon, cloves and nutmeg. Use *whole berries* for boiling fish; in stews; meat marinades; spiced fruit; chutneys (tied in muslin); pickles. Use *ground* in soups; vegetable dishes; steamed dried fruit puddings; with baked bananas, figs, pineapple; in fruit cakes; black bun; biscuits; relishes; chutneys.

Anise Seed Liquorice flavour. Use *whole seeds* in fish chowders; meat stews; with vegetables — particularly green and red cabbage, carrots, turnips, beetroot, cauliflower; scattered over rolls and bread; in milk and non-alcoholic drinks. Use *ground* in soups; fish dishes; marinades; cold sweets; fancy breads; cakes; biscuits.

Caraway Seed Distinct liquorice flavour, stronger than anise. Use *whole seeds* in dumplings for soups and stews; in meat stews; with liver; pork; goulash; vegetables — particularly red and white cabbage, cauliflower, beetroot, turnips, potatoes; in rye and other breads; biscuits and cookies; cheese; pickles. Use *ground* in stews; with vegetables — particularly courgettes, beans, cabbage, tomatoes, potato salad, chicory.

Cardamom Distinctive warm, slightly pungent aromatic flavour. Use *whole seed pods* in rice dishes; pickles (tied in muslin); spiced wine and punches; coffee. Use *ground* in curries; meat loaves; American hamburgers; baked apples and apple pie;

Sorrel French

pumpkin pie; scattered over melon; in spiced fruit salad; Danish pastries, cakes and buns; Swedish cakes.

Cayenne See Capsicum (page 28). Cayenne pepper is traditionally the hottest of all spices, chilli powder coming second. An essential ingredient of curries and curry powder. Use in shellfish and fish dishes; egg dishes; devilled meat, particularly chicken, turkey, kidneys, sausages; devilled sauces; vegetable dishes; cheese dishes and any savoury dish which needs pepping up.

Chilli Powder See Capsicum (page 28). Chilli (spelt with two ll's) powder in India and other tropical countries refers to the powder ground from small, very hot red chillies. Chili (spelt with one l) powder, the American condiment, is a blend of spices including the basic ground chillis. It is not as hot as cayenne and is used extensively for Mexican dishes; in cocktail sauces for shellfish; minced meat; etc. It is interchangeable with cayenne.

Cinnamon and Cassia True cinnamon has a more delicate sweet, spicy flavour than cassia, which is more pungent with a 'bite' on the tongue. Use *sticks* of cinnamon for cooking apples, prunes, oranges; in spiced fruit for serving with poultry and meat; in rice dishes; spiced wine cups; pickling vinegars. Use *ground* in spiced hot grapefruit; meat dishes; vegetable dishes; stewed fruits such as apples, bananas, oranges, prunes; fruit pies; pumpkin pie; for topping milk and custard puddings; as cinnamon toast. Use cassia *bark* for spiced meat dishes; curries; rice dishes.

Cloves Sharp, spicy, strong flavour. Use *whole* stuck into an onion for soup and sauce making; for studding baked ham; in boiling beef; spiced tongue; beetroot salad; pickled vegetables; baked and stewed fruit; spiced fruit; apple and bread sauces; punches; mulled ale. Use *ground* in meat stews; curries; mincemeat; with vegetables — particularly beetroot, sweet potatoes, chicory; in fruit pies; pumpkin pies; spiced fruit; cakes; buns; biscuits and cookies.

Coriander Mild, resembles mixture of orange, lemon, anise and cumin. As it is so mild, use more in proportion to other spices. Use *whole seeds* in pickled fish; curries; pickled vegetables; in any dish 'à la Grecque'. Use *ground* in soups; fish dishes; meat stews; curries; roast and pork dishes; chicken dishes; sausage dishes; stuffings; lentil dishes; milk puddings and custards; cakes; cookies; Eastern sweets.

Cumin (Jeera) Strong, aromatic, distinctive flavour. Use *whole seeds* in curries; meat stews; Mexican dishes; sauerkraut; cheese dishes; chutney. Use *ground* in soups; fish dishes; meat loaves; pork dishes; curries; Mexican and Turkish dishes; stuffed vegetables — particularly aubergine, peppers, tomatoes; dried bean dishes; sauces; cheese dishes.

Fenugreek Strong flavour with a background of bitterness. Use *ground* in vegetable and bean soups; curries; meat stews; pickles; chutneys.

Ginger Strong, hot flavour. Use *fresh* (green) or from cans in Chinese fish and meat dishes; fish dishes; with vegetables such as onions and artichokes; dried beans; in curries; stews. Use *whole dried root* (rhizome) in pickles and chutneys (tied in muslin); pickling vinegars; home-made ginger beer and ginger wine. Use *ground* scattered over melon and grapefruit; in soups; fish dishes; chicken dishes; meat stews; vegetable dishes; sweet sauces; fruit pies; pumpkin pie; stewed fruit; gingerbreads; cakes; biscuits and cookies; chutneys.

Juniper Berries Strong, bitter-sweet, rather astringent flavour. Use *crushed* in pâtés; with venison, rabbit, hare, braised pigeon and other game; hearts; pork; in a variety of meat dishes; in stuffings for poultry, duck, goose.

Mace Strong, warm, sweet and spicy flavour. Rather stronger than nutmeg. Use *blades* in soups; rice dishes; sauces; pickling; hot punches and fruit cups. Use *ground* in soups; fish and shellfish dishes; veal stews; sauces; cakes; cookies; pastries.

Mustard Strong, hot, pungent flavour. The dry powder is bitter before liquid is added. Use *whole seeds* in boiled beetroot, cabbage, sauerkraut; in pickling; pickles; chutneys. Use *powder* in fish dishes; poultry dishes; meat dishes; devilled dishes; sauces; egg dishes; cheese dishes; mayonnaise; salad dressings; like curry powder with any food which needs pepping up.

Note: Apart from hot English mustard, which is made from the black (brown) and white (yellow) mustard seed varieties, there are countless made-up mustards which each have their individual flavour and appeal.

Nutmeg Strong, sweet and spicy flavour. Similar to mace but rather less strong. Use *grated* (fresh is best, but it can be bought already ground) in soups; fish dishes; meat dishes; with tripe; in sausage dishes; pies — savoury and sweet; with vegetables — particularly cauliflower, cabbage, spinach, carrots, cucumber, chicory; in sauces; egg dishes; over milk puddings and custards; in junkets; steamed and baked puddings; biscuits and cookies; fruit cakes; egg nogs; in mixtures of spices.

Paprika See Capsicum (page 28). Mild, sweet, non-pungent, brilliant red. Use in soups; fish dishes; with veal; lamb; in sausage dishes; goulash; beef dishes; chicken dishes; Spanish dishes; with pasta; in sauces; cheese dishes; as garnish for eye appeal over cheese, egg, potato, cauliflower or any pale coloured dish.

Pepper Black pepper has a strong, hot, more pungent flavour than white pepper. Use *whole peppercorns* in marinades for fish and meat; in boiled beef; boiled mutton; with gammon; in pickling (often tied in muslin). It is very important to grind freshly from a pepper mill both in the kitchen and at the table. Use *ground* black pepper in almost all savoury dishes. Use white for pale coloured food where black would appear as unpleasant dark specks.

Poppy Seed Delightful crunchy, nutty flavour. Use *whole seeds* in curries; with rice or pasta; in cakes; biscuits; pastry; cheese canapés; for toppings on rolls and breads. Use *crushed* mixed with sugar and honey or syrup as filling for pastries or cakes.

Saffron Pleasantly bitter, distinctive flavour. Prepare as described (see page 35). Use in bouillabaisse, dried bean and other soups; in fish and shellfish dishes; paella; rice dishes; chicken dishes; sauces; breads; cakes.

Sesame Seed Crisp, nut-like flavour. Use *untoasted* scattered over breads, rolls, cookies and biscuits. Use *toasted* (in the oven to a pale brown) in vegetable dishes; over salads; pastries; with cream cheese; in any dish in place of expensive nuts. *Tahini* (a runny paste made from finely ground seeds and sold in jars) is used for Arab dishes such as *hoummos, moutabal,* etc.

Turmeric Distinctive delicate, aromatic flavour. Use *ground* in fish and shellfish dishes; curries; stews; rice dishes; vegetable dishes; sauces; pickles such as piccalilli; chutneys.

Vanilla Sweet and permeating flavour and scent. Use *beans* for sweets and cakes as vanilla sugar. Use *essence* in chocolate and coffee sweets; puddings; cakes; biscuits and cookies; with fruit; in ice cream; custards and milk puddings; sweet sauces; hot chocolate drinks; candies.

Curried Apple and Sausage Soup with Rice Pancakes (see page 51)
Overleaf: Stuffed Egg Salad (see page 51)

Recipes

Cooking with herbs and spices can become an insidious habit. Once the first voyage of discovery in the kitchen has been navigated successfully, no cook will ever want to be without either a well-stocked spice rack or a freezer containing at least her favourite herbs.

I have always been enthralled with the flavours of the herb and spice ingredients encountered in the different parts of the world I have visited.

All herbs can be grown in temperate climates and in the Western world can, therefore, be enjoyed in their pristine freshness. But almost all the spices prefer tropical temperatures, so in colder climates we must be content with the dried varieties.

For their invaluable help to me my grateful thanks go to:

The Royal Horticultural Society's Garden, Wisley, Ripley, Woking, Surrey.

Mr. and Mrs. R. E. Hawkins, The Old Coach House Nurseries, Norton-sub-Hamdon, Somerset.

McCormick Foods (UK) Ltd., P.O. Box 5, Ellesmere Port, South Wirral L65 3DA.

Schwartz Spice Information Bureau, 6 Cavendish Square, London W1M 9HA.

Cooking notes

It is always difficult to convey one's reasons for doing one thing and not doing something else. But so the reader may understand as many of my reasons as possible, I would like to mention a few points.

1. I have not used composite spices and seasonings because most are hard to find outside large towns. The only ones which are fairly universal are seasoned salt and seasoned pepper, so these make a few appearances. However, this should not deter anybody who feels like trying the more exotic mixtures. They are fun, often delicious and well worth an experiment.

2. Where the word 'fresh' for a herb is specified it is much superior to dried for that particular dish, but half the quantity of the dried variety can always be substituted unless categorically barred. In general, when unspecified, herbs used are dried.

3. Wherever butter is mentioned, margarine can be substituted. It is up to the reader to decide whether the additional flavour from butter warrants the extra cost and calories.

4. All oven temperatures and timing are taken from the centre shelf unless otherwise stated.

5. Where a recipe calls for simmering in the oven, the oven temperature is never given as it will depend on the type of casserole dish used.

Bacon and Cauliflower Soup (see page 49)

Soups and Starters

Bilberry Soup

SERVES 6

METRIC/IMPERIAL	AMERICAN
450 g/1 lb bilberries	1 lb blueberries
900 ml/1½ pints water	3¾ cups water
½ teaspoon ground cinnamon	½ teaspoon ground cinnamon
½ teaspoon sweet cicely (optional)	½ teaspoon sweet cicely (optional)
50-75 g/2-3 oz sugar	4-6 tablespoons sugar
½ tablespoon cornflour	½ tablespoon cornstarch
150 ml/5 fl oz double or single cream	⅔ cup whipping or coffee cream

Wash the bilberries. Bring the water, cinnamon and sweet cicely, if used, to the boil. Add the fruit and 50 g/2 oz (us 4 tablespoons) of the sugar and boil for 3-4 minutes until the fruit is tender. Pulp in a blender or rub through a sieve.

Mix the cornflour to a smooth paste with a little of the soup, return to the pan, taste and add more sugar if necessary. Bring to the boil, stirring, and boil for a minute or so. Pour into bowls and swirl a tablespoon or more of cream into each if serving hot. Or chill before adding cream, for serving cold.

Chilled Tomato Soup

SERVES 4

METRIC/IMPERIAL	AMERICAN
1 kg/2 lb tomatoes	2 lb tomatoes
1 tablespoon chopped onion	1 tablespoon chopped onion
1 teaspoon fresh tarragon	1 teaspoon fresh tarragon
½ tablespoon tomato purée or ketchup	½ tablespoon tomato paste or catsup
2 teaspoons sugar	2 teaspoons sugar
1 teaspoon salt	1 teaspoon salt
pepper	pepper
150 ml/5 fl oz double or soured cream	⅔ cup whipping or sour cream
chopped chives or parsley	chopped chives or parsley

Wash and quarter the tomatoes. Purée the tomatoes, onion and tarragon in a blender until smooth then rub through a fine sieve, or rub through a sieve by hand. Stir in the tomato purée thoroughly with the sugar, salt and pepper to taste. Chill.

To serve, stir in the cream, pour into soup bowls and garnish with chopped chives or parsley.

Clear Bortsch

SERVES 4-5

METRIC/IMPERIAL	AMERICAN
675 g-1 kg/1½-2 lb raw beetroot (small red kind)	1½-2 lb raw beets
1.15 litres/2 pints beef stock (or water and 2 stock cubes)	5 cups beef stock (or water and 2 bouillon cubes)
¼ teaspoon dill or fennel seeds	¼ teaspoon dill or fennel seeds
salt and pepper	salt and pepper
Smetana or soured cream	Smetana or sour cream
chopped chives or parsley	chopped chives or parsley

Peel and grate the beetroot coarsely. Add to the stock and bring to the boil with the seeds and salt and pepper to taste (according to the stock used). Simmer for 40-50 minutes, then strain through a piece of muslin over a strainer.

To serve, bring to boiling point and pour into soup bowls, add a good spoonful of Smetana or soured cream to each bowl and sprinkle with chopped chives or parsley.

Consommé Celestine

SERVES 5-6

This soup is named after Saint Celestine who, in 1294, became Pope Celestine V and was later canonised. The herbed pancakes which are its feature can be made a day ahead and kept wrapped. The consommé out of a can is almost as good with a tablespoon or two of dry sherry stirred in.

METRIC/IMPERIAL	AMERICAN
1 tablespoon grated Parmesan cheese	1 tablespoon grated Parmesan cheese
½ teaspoon chopped chervil	½ teaspoon chopped chervil
½ teaspoon chopped tarragon	½ teaspoon chopped tarragon
1 teaspoon chopped parsley	1 teaspoon chopped parsley
salt	salt
50 g/2 oz plain flour	½ cup all-purpose flour
1 egg	1 egg
150 ml/¼ pint milk	⅔ cup milk
1.15 litres/2 pints boiling consommé	5 cups boiling consommé

Stir the cheese, herbs and salt into the flour. Mix into a batter with the egg and milk and fry the pancakes. Cut into thin strips. Place as many strips as desired in a soup tureen or bowls, pour over the boiling consommé and serve immediately.

Crème du Barry

SERVES 5-6

Comtesse (known usually as Madame) du Barry was the famous mistress of Louis XV, who awarded the Comtesse's woman chef the title 'Cordon Bleu'. Madame du Barry must have been excessively fond of cauliflower, for as a garnish her name denotes cauliflower in some form. The best known of the dishes named after her is this soup.

METRIC/IMPERIAL	AMERICAN
450 g/1 lb cauliflower (without leaves)	1 lb cauliflower (without leaves)
150-175 g/5-6 oz potatoes, peeled	⅓ lb potatoes, peeled
750 ml/1¼ pints water	3 cups water
salt and pepper	salt and pepper
¼ teaspoon grated nutmeg	¼ teaspoon grated nutmeg
375 ml/13 fl oz milk	approx. 1½ cups milk
15 g/½ oz butter	1 tablespoon butter

Cut the cauliflower and potatoes into rough pieces, add the water and bring to the boil with 2 teaspoons salt. Simmer, covered, for 30 minutes, then purée in a blender or rub through a sieve. Add the nutmeg and milk, adjust seasoning and boil for 2-3 minutes. Remove from the heat and stir in the butter gradually. Serve with fried croûtons of bread.

Gazpacho Andaluz

SERVES 6

This famous Spanish soup can be made in dozens of different ways. The version I give here is the one I learned in Andalucia; I thought it was one of the nicest I had tasted.

METRIC/IMPERIAL	AMERICAN
50 g/2 oz crustless white bread	2 slices crustless white bread
900 ml/1½ pints water	3¾ cups water
675 g/1½ lb tomatoes, skinned	1½ lb tomatoes, skinned
1 medium cucumber	1 medium cucumber
1 green pepper	1 green pepper
1 medium onion, peeled	1 medium onion, peeled
1-2 cloves garlic, chopped and crushed	1-2 cloves garlic, chopped and crushed
½ teaspoon ground cumin	½ teaspoon ground cumin
3 tablespoons wine vinegar	¼ cup wine vinegar
1 teaspoon salt	1 teaspoon salt

Soak the roughly crumbled bread in one-third of the water until soft, then beat it up. Roughly chop the vegetables and stir in with the rest of the ingredients; leave to soak for at least 3-4 hours or overnight.

Purée the mixture in a blender then rub through a fine sieve. Chill thoroughly.

To serve, hand the following items separately, all finely cubed: 1 green pepper; 225 g/8 oz (US ½ lb) tomatoes, skinned and seeded; ½ cucumber, unpeeled; 2 slices bread from a sliced sandwich loaf, crusts removed.

Bacon and Cauliflower Soup

SERVES 4

METRIC/IMPERIAL	AMERICAN
1 kg/2 lb bacon or gammon knuckle	2 lb smoked shoulder butt or knuckle
1.15 litres/2 pints water	2½ pints water
275-350 g/10-12 oz cauliflower florets	⅔-¾ lb cauliflower florets
1½ teaspoons fresh or ½ teaspoon dried thyme	1½ teaspoons fresh or ½ teaspoon dried thyme
100 g/4 oz onion, sliced	1 cup sliced onion
1 tablespoon oil	1 tablespoon oil
300 ml/½ pint milk	1¼ cups milk
75 g/3 oz soft breadcrumbs	1½ cups soft bread crumbs
salt and pepper	salt and pepper
chopped parsley (optional)	chopped parsley (optional)

Place the knuckle in the water and bring to the boil; skim and boil, covered, for 45 minutes-1 hour. Remove the knuckle and cut off the meat into chunks.

Strain 750 ml/1¼ pints (US 1½ pints) of the stock into a saucepan and add the cauliflower and thyme (reserving a floret and a few leaves of thyme for garnish). Bring to the boil and boil, covered, for 15 minutes. Blend in a liquidiser or rub through a sieve.

Fry the onion in the oil without allowing it to colour and add to the saucepan with the cauliflower purée and the milk, breadcrumbs and meat. Simmer for 20 minutes. Add a little more milk if a thinner soup is desired. Season with salt, if necessary, and pepper. Garnish with the reserved cauliflower floret and scatter over the reserved thyme leaves or chopped parsley.

(Illustrated on page 46.)

Sopa Triton

SERVES 4

I was taught this delicious soup by Chef Alfredo Diz of the Triton Hotel in Torremolinos on Spain's Costa del Sol.

METRIC/IMPERIAL	AMERICAN
1 small leek, very finely chopped	1 small leek, very finely chopped
1 small carrot, very finely chopped	1 small carrot, very finely chopped
1½ tablespoons chopped fresh or ¾ tablespoon dried tarragon	2 tablespoons chopped fresh or ¾ tablespoon dried tarragon
25 g/1 oz butter	2 tablespoons butter
300 ml/½ pint chicken stock	1¼ cups chicken stock
225-250 g/8-9 oz potatoes, peeled	generous ½ lb potatoes, peeled
1 egg yolk	1 egg yolk
300 ml/10 fl oz single cream	1¼ cups coffee cream
salt and pepper	salt and pepper

Fry the leek, carrot and tarragon in the butter for 5-7 minutes until fairly soft. Remove from the heat and stir in the stock.

Boil the potatoes and mash well (better still, rub through a sieve). Beat in the egg yolk thoroughly. Stir in the cream then the vegetables. Season to taste. Chill well and stir before serving.

Sinhalese Soup

SERVES 4

The lovely Cyd Charisse has the graceful svelte lines of a former ballerina, yet still enjoys food. Particularly fond is she of soups — hot and cold. And this adaptation of Mulligatawny can be served hot or cold.

METRIC/IMPERIAL	AMERICAN
½ onion, peeled	½ onion, peeled
1 clove garlic	1 clove garlic
175 g/6 oz tomatoes	⅓ lb tomatoes
1 medium cooking apple	1 medium baking apple
15 g/½ oz butter	1 tablespoon butter
1 tablespoon oil	1 tablespoon oil
½ tablespoon curry powder	½ tablespoon curry powder
½ teaspoon ground cumin	½ teaspoon ground cumin
¼ teaspoon ground turmeric	¼ teaspoon ground turmeric
½ teaspoon salt	½ teaspoon salt
25 g/1 oz flour	¼ cup all-purpose flour
1.15 litres/2 pints chicken stock (or water and 2 stock cubes)	5 cups chicken stock (or water and 2 bouillon cubes)
½ tablespoon lemon juice	½ tablespoon lemon juice

Slice the onion finely, peel, chop and crush the garlic, skin and chop the tomatoes and chop half the unpeeled apple.

In a thick-bottomed saucepan, gently fry the onion and garlic in the butter and oil until golden. Add the tomato, chopped apple, spices, and salt; cover and allow to sweat for about 5 minutes, stirring occasionally.

Make the flour into a paste with a little of the stock, add to the pan with the rest of the stock and boil gently, uncovered, for 30 minutes. Put through a blender or rub through a sieve. Stir in the lemon juice, adjust seasoning and add the rest of the apple, peeled and grated on a medium grater.

Green Pepper Summer Cream

SERVES 4

METRIC/IMPERIAL	AMERICAN
1 large or 2 small green peppers	1 large or 2 small green peppers
750 ml/1¼ pints chicken stock	3 cups chicken stock
1 teaspoon mixed herbs	1 teaspoon mixed herbs
½ tablespoon cornflour	½ tablespoon cornstarch
½ tablespoon cold water	½ tablespoon cold water
150 ml/5 fl oz soured cream or yogurt	⅔ cup sour cream or yogurt
chopped parsley	chopped parsley

Wash the peppers, remove the stalks and seeds and chop the flesh roughly. Put with the stock and herbs in a pan, bring to the boil and simmer, covered, for 40-45 minutes. Turn into a blender until smooth, then pour through a sieve into a saucepan, or rub through a sieve by hand.

Make the cornflour into a paste with the water and stir into the soup. Bring to the boil, stirring, and boil for 2-3 minutes. Leave to cool then stir in the soured cream, season if necessary and chill. Serve garnished with chopped parsley.

Giblet Soup

SERVES 5

An excellent way to finish off leftover poultry after a party.

METRIC/IMPERIAL	AMERICAN
giblets from 2 chickens or ducks	giblets from 2 chickens or ducks
1.4 litres/2½ pints bird stock	6¼ cups bird stock
½ onion, peeled	½ onion, peeled
2 small carrots, peeled	2 small carrots, peeled
bouquet garni or 1 teaspoon mixed herbs	bouquet garni or 1 teaspoon mixed herbs
salt and pepper	salt and pepper
25 g/1 oz flour	¼ cup all-purpose flour
1-2 tablespoons port (optional)	1-3 tablespoons port (optional)
chopped parsley	chopped parsley

Wash the giblets thoroughly, remove all the fat and cut the meat into pieces. Turn into a pan with the necks and the stock. Bring to the boil, skim well, then add the roughly chopped onion and carrot, herbs, and salt and pepper to taste. Simmer, covered, for 1½-2 hours until the giblets are quite tender. Cut all the meat off the necks and then put through a blender or rub through a sieve.

Make the flour into a paste with a little of the soup and stir into the pan. Bring to the boil, stirring, and boil for 3-4 minutes. Stir in the port, if used, just before serving and sprinkle with chopped parsley.

Almond Soup

SERVES 4

A delightful accompaniment to this soup is yellow rice (see page 85), served separately so that each person can add as much as they like.

METRIC/IMPERIAL	AMERICAN
125 g/4½ oz ground almonds	1 cup ground almonds
250 ml/8 fl oz milk	1 cup milk
25 g/1 oz soft breadcrumbs	½ cup soft bread crumbs
15 g/½ oz butter	1 tablespoon butter
25 g/1 oz flour	¼ cup all-purpose flour
750 ml/1¼ pints chicken stock	3 cups chicken stock
generous ¼ teaspoon ground mace	generous ¼ teaspoon ground mace
4 tablespoons cream	⅓ cup cream
salt and white pepper	salt and white pepper
chopped parsley	chopped parsley

Turn the almonds, milk, and breadcrumbs into a saucepan and bring just to boiling point, stirring. Remove from the heat.

Melt the butter in a large saucepan and stir in the flour and the almond mixture. Gradually blend in the stock and mace. Bring to the boil and simmer gently for 5 minutes. Stir in the cream and season to taste with salt and pepper. Pour into a soup tureen or four bowls and sprinkle liberally with chopped parsley.

Potato Chervil Soup

SERVES 4-5

A particularly delicious soup to serve for supper or as a 'warmer-upper' after an evening's outing. The time and trouble can be cut considerably by using an instant potato powder in place of the raw potato. In that case, increase the stock to 1.15 litres/2 pints (US 5 cups) and simmer for 10-15 minutes only, then sprinkle the contents of a large (142-g/5-oz) packet of instant potato on to the boiling liquid and stir thoroughly. Finish off as below.

The chervil must not be cooked or it will lose much of its flavour, so add it only after the soup has been removed from the heat.

METRIC/IMPERIAL	AMERICAN
450 g/1 lb potatoes, after peeling	1 lb potatoes, after peeling
1 small onion, peeled	1 small onion, peeled
25 g/1 oz butter	2 tablespoons butter
900 ml/1½ pints white stock	3¾ cups white stock
1 small bay leaf	1 small bay leaf
⅛ teaspoon ground mace	⅛ teaspoon ground mace
150 ml/5 fl oz single cream or milk	⅔ cup coffee cream or milk
salt and pepper	salt and pepper
5-6 tablespoons chopped chervil	6-7 tablespoons chopped chervil

Slice the potatoes and onion. Melt the butter and sweat the vegetables gently with the pan covered, stirring occasionally, for 8-10 minutes. Pour in the stock. Add the bay leaf and mace and simmer, covered, for 45-50 minutes.

Remove the bay leaf and put the soup through a blender or rub through a sieve. Stir in the cream or milk and season to taste with salt and pepper. Reheat, then remove from the heat and stir in the chervil. Serve with fried croûtons, if liked.

Curried Apple and Sausage Soup with Rice Pancakes

SERVES 4

Although this is a soup to be eaten with a spoon, served with these unusual rice pancakes it makes a tasty main dish.

METRIC/IMPERIAL	AMERICAN
100 g/4 oz onion, coarsely chopped	1 cup coarsely chopped onion
25 g/1 oz butter	2 tablespoons butter
2 tablespoons oil	3 tablespoons oil
1 tablespoon curry powder	1 tablespoon curry powder
25 g/1 oz flour	¼ cup all-purpose flour
2 tablespoons mango chutney	3 tablespoons mango chutney
1 tablespoon tomato purée	1 tablespoon tomato paste
750 ml/1¼ pints stock (or water and 2 stock cubes)	3 cups stock (or water and 2 bouillon cubes)
225 g/8 oz skinless or other sausages	½ lb skinless or other sausages
2 crisp apples	2 crisp apples
salt	salt

Gently fry the onion in the butter and oil until beginning to brown then add the curry powder, fry for a minute or two and blend in the flour thoroughly. Gradually add the chutney, tomato purée and the stock; cover and simmer for 20 minutes.

Meanwhile grill the sausages and cut into pieces. Peel, core and cut the apples into pieces 5 mm-1 cm/¼-½ inch thick. Turn both into the soup and simmer for 5 minutes more. Season to taste with salt.

Rice Pancakes

METRIC/IMPERIAL	AMERICAN
75 g/3 oz raw rice	⅓ cup raw rice
125 g/4½ oz plain flour	generous cup all-purpose flour
1½ teaspoons curry powder	1½ teaspoons curry powder
½ teaspoon salt	½ teaspoon salt
1 egg, beaten	1 egg, beaten
1 teaspoon soy sauce	1 teaspoon soy sauce
approx. 300 ml/½ pint milk	approx. 1¼ cups milk
oil	oil

Cook the rice in boiling salted water until tender. Drain. Stir in the flour, curry powder, salt, beaten egg, soy sauce and sufficient milk to give a thin batter.

Heat a little oil in a small frying pan and pour in enough batter to just cover the base. Fry until golden brown on the underside, flip over and cook the second side. Repeat with remaining batter, adding more oil to the pan if necessary.

Top the pancakes with a spoonful of mango chutney, if liked, and serve soy sauce separately. *(Illustrated on page 43.)*

Stuffed Egg Salad

SERVES 4

METRIC/IMPERIAL	AMERICAN
4 hard-boiled eggs	4 hard-cooked eggs
1½ tablespoons mayonnaise	2 tablespoons mayonnaise
40 g/1½ oz soft margarine	3 tablespoons soft margarine
2 tablespoons (firmly packed) chopped fresh mixed herbs	3 tablespoons (firmly packed) chopped fresh mixed herbs
salt and pepper	salt and pepper
225 g/8 oz frozen peas, lightly cooked	1½ cups frozen peas, lightly cooked
spring onions, chopped	scallions, chopped
4 tablespoons French dressing	⅓ cup French dressing
175 g/6 oz cooked long-grain rice	1 cup cooked long-grain rice
1 lemon, sliced lengthways	1 lemon, sliced lengthwise
1 bunch watercress	1 bunch watercress

Cut the eggs in half lengthways and scoop out the yolks. Mash the yolks with a fork and beat in the mayonnaise, margarine and mixed herbs. Season to taste. Pile back into the whites, mounding the tops.

Mix the peas, chopped spring onions to taste and French dressing into the rice. Turn on to a serving dish, arrange the stuffed eggs on top with slices of lemon between them, and surround with watercress. *(Illustrated on pages 44-45.)*

Sausage and Mushroom Minarets

SERVES 8

If these sausage cakes are not to be garnished, 175 g/6 oz (US 1½ cups) mushrooms of any kind will be sufficient.

METRIC/IMPERIAL	AMERICAN
225 g/8 oz button mushrooms	2 cups button mushrooms
450 g/1 lb sausagemeat	2 cups sausagemeat
1 teaspoon oregano	1 teaspoon oregano
1 tablespoon chopped parsley	1 tablespoon chopped parsley
½ teaspoon seasoned salt	½ teaspoon seasoned salt
1 egg, beaten	1 egg, beaten
1 (99-g/3½-oz) packet sage and onion stuffing mix	1 (3½-oz) package sage and onion stuffing mix
oil	oil
butter (optional)	butter (optional)
salt and pepper	salt and pepper
tomato and cucumber slices	tomato and cucumber slices

Wash the mushrooms quickly and wipe dry. Reserve 16 or 24 small ones for garnishing and chop the rest finely. Mix into the sausagemeat with the herbs and seasoned salt.

Divide the mixture into eight equal portions and pat each into a neat cake. Brush with beaten egg and coat with the dry stuffing. Leave to dry before frying. Fry gently in oil until nicely browned on both sides. Lightly fry the reserved mushrooms in butter or oil and season with salt and pepper. Place slices of tomato or cucumber on each cake and stick a skewer or cocktail stick through them, spiked with 2-3 whole mushrooms.

(Illustrated on page 91.)

Norwegian Sea-fruit Cocktail

SERVES 4

METRIC/IMPERIAL	AMERICAN
100-175 g/4-6 oz fresh peeled or frozen prawns	¼-⅓ lb fresh shelled or frozen shrimp
½ cantaloup or honeydew melon	½ cantaloup or honeydew melon
1½ tablespoons cream	2 tablespoons cream
½-¾ teaspoon curry powder	½-¾ teaspoon curry powder
¼ teaspoon paprika	¼ teaspoon paprika
4 tablespoons mayonnaise	5 tablespoons mayonnaise
salt	salt
sprigs of dill or mint leaves	sprigs of dill or mint leaves

If the prawns are frozen, allow them to thaw out thoroughly. Reserve four for garnish. Cut the flesh of the melon into balls with a melon baller or into small cubes and reserve four of these.

Beat the cream, curry powder and paprika into the mayonnaise and season with salt to taste.

Turn the prawns and melon into four shallow sundae glasses and spoon over the sauce. Garnish each with a reserved prawn, melon ball or cube and a sprig of dill, or one or two mint leaves.

Salad Vegetables with Paprika Mayonnaise

This is an attractive way of serving a vegetable salad, either as a starter or refreshments for a drinks party.

Mix sufficient paprika into mayonnaise to give a delicate pink colour, then stir in cayenne and salt to taste. Turn into a bowl, sprinkle with paprika and surround with neatly cut vegetables.

Crab and Mushroom Mousse

SERVES 4 (OR 6 AS STARTER)

This is not meant to be a completely smooth mousse; it's rather nice to taste the little pieces of crabmeat. If shell moulds are not available, set the mixture in a 20-cm/8-inch ring mould and garnish in the same manner.

METRIC/IMPERIAL	AMERICAN
1 (800-g-1-kg/1¾-2-lb) fresh crab, cooked, or 225 g/8 oz frozen crabmeat	1 (1¾-2-lb) fresh crab, cooked, or ½ lb frozen crabmeat
175 g/6 oz button mushrooms	1½ cups button mushrooms
salt and pepper	salt and pepper
15 g/½ oz butter	1 tablespoon butter
3 tablespoons boiling water	4 tablespoons boiling water
2 teaspoons gelatine	2 teaspoons gelatin
3 tablespoons mayonnaise	4 tablespoons mayonnaise
2 tablespoons lemon juice	3 tablespoons lemon juice
1 teaspoon made English mustard	1 teaspoon prepared English mustard
1 teaspoon anchovy essence	1 teaspoon anchovy extract
1 tablespoon chopped chives	1 tablespoon chopped chives
1 tablespoon chopped parsley	1 tablespoon chopped parsley
250 ml/8 fl oz double cream	1 cup whipping cream
sprigs of dill, fennel or watercress	sprigs of dill, fennel or watercress

Keeping the small claws intact, remove all the meat from the crab, if used, discarding any bone, and flake the meat. Wash, dry and chop the mushrooms finely. Season with salt and pepper. Gently simmer the crabmeat and mushrooms in the butter in a small saucepan for 2-3 minutes only. Drain.

Pour the boiling water over the gelatine in a cup and stir occasionally until completely melted and smooth. Mix the mayonnaise, lemon juice, mustard, anchovy essence and herbs together and stir in the gelatine. Whip the cream and add to the mixture with the crabmeat and mushrooms. Turn into the moulds, which have been rinsed out with cold water or oiled, and leave to set in the refrigerator.

Turn out and garnish with the small claws and/or sprigs of dill, fennel or watercress.

(Illustrated on page 34.)

Mushrooms à la Grecque

SERVES 4

This dish can be served on its own as a first course, or as one of several for an hors d'oeuvre for six to eight people.

METRIC/IMPERIAL	AMERICAN
225 g/8 oz small button mushrooms	2 cups small button mushrooms
1 (227-g/8-oz) can tomatoes	1 (8-oz) can tomatoes
$\frac{1}{2}$ onion, peeled	$\frac{1}{2}$ onion, peeled
150 ml/$\frac{1}{4}$ pint olive oil	$\frac{2}{3}$ cup olive oil
2 sprigs of thyme	2 sprigs of thyme
$\frac{1}{2}$ bay leaf	$\frac{1}{2}$ bay leaf
6 peppercorns, lightly crushed	6 peppercorns, lightly crushed
$\frac{1}{2}$ teaspoon salt	$\frac{1}{2}$ teaspoon salt

Wash and dry the mushrooms and cut any larger ones in half. Rub the tomatoes through a sieve. Slice the onion lengthways, fairly thinly. Heat the oil in a saucepan, turn all the ingredients into it, cover and simmer until tender, about 10 minutes. Serve cold.

French Rice Salad

SERVES 4-5

Serve this salad in sundae glasses as a first course. For a main course salad, increase the quantities by about a third and pile into a large bowl.

METRIC/IMPERIAL	AMERICAN
100 g/4 oz long-grain rice	$\frac{1}{2}$ cup long-grain rice
salt	salt
50 g/2 oz blue cheese	$\frac{1}{2}$ cup crumbled blue cheese
2 teaspoons lemon juice	2 teaspoons lemon juice
150 ml/5 fl oz soured cream	$\frac{2}{3}$ cup sour cream
2 sticks celery	2 stalks celery
10-12 radishes (optional)	10-12 radishes (optional)
5-cm/2-inch piece cucumber	2-inch piece cucumber
225-275 g/8-10 oz tomatoes	approx. $\frac{1}{2}$ lb tomatoes
1$\frac{1}{2}$ teaspoons chopped fresh dill (or $\frac{3}{4}$ teaspoon dill weed)	1$\frac{1}{2}$ teaspoons chopped fresh dill (or $\frac{3}{4}$ teaspoon dill weed)
2 teaspoons chopped fresh or 1$\frac{1}{4}$ teaspoons dried marjoram	2 teaspoons chopped fresh or 1$\frac{1}{4}$ teaspoons dried marjoram
$\frac{3}{4}$-1 tablespoon chopped chives	$\frac{3}{4}$-1 tablespoon chopped chives

Drop the rice into boiling, salted water and boil for 15-18 minutes, until the rice is tender but still retains a slight 'bite' in the centre. Drain well. Or cook by the absorption method: put rice, 300 ml/$\frac{1}{2}$ pint (US 1$\frac{1}{4}$ cups) water and $\frac{1}{2}$ teaspoon salt into a saucepan. Bring to the boil and stir, cover and simmer for 15-18 minutes or until all the liquid has been absorbed.

Crumble the cheese roughly and mix with the lemon juice and soured cream. Wash and finely slice the celery and radishes, if used, and cut the unpeeled cucumber into 5-mm/$\frac{1}{4}$-inch cubes. Cut the tomatoes into wedges, keep some aside for garnish

and chop the rest. Mix the vegetables, rice and herbs together and pile into sundae glasses.

Put a spoonful of the soured cream dressing on top of each. Garnish with the reserved tomato wedges and a sprig of dill if available.

Karrysalat

SERVES 4-5

This Danish salad makes a delicious lunch or supper dish, and the sauce can also be used for other cold dishes.

METRIC/IMPERIAL	AMERICAN
225 g/8 oz pasta shells or short-cut macaroni	$\frac{1}{2}$ lb shell or other macaroni
4-5 tablespoons French dressing	5-6 tablespoons French dressing
2 dessert apples, cored and sliced	2 dessert apples, cored and sliced
50 g/2 oz seedless raisins	$\frac{1}{3}$ cup seedless raisins
salt and pepper	salt and pepper
2 (198-g/7-oz) cans fresh herrings or 4 rollmops	2 (7-oz) cans fresh herrings or 4 rollmops
1 tablespoon hot curry powder	1 tablespoon hot curry powder
grated rind and juice of $\frac{1}{2}$ lemon	grated rind and juice of $\frac{1}{2}$ lemon
2 tablespoons chopped parsley	3 tablespoons chopped parsley
300 ml/10 fl oz soured cream	1$\frac{1}{4}$ cups sour cream

Drop the pasta into boiling salted water and boil until just tender, 13-15 minutes. Drain, return to the saucepan and stir in the French dressing at once. Add the apple slices and raisins and season to taste with salt and pepper. Turn into a shallow dish and place the fish, cut in pieces, on top.

Stir the curry powder, lemon rind and juice and the chopped parsley into the soured cream, season with more salt and spoon over the fish.

(Illustrated on page 92.)

Fish

Cod's Roe Pie
SERVES 4-5

METRIC/IMPERIAL	AMERICAN
450 g/1 lb cooked cod's roe	1 lb cooked cod's roe
50 g/2 oz onion, finely chopped	½ cup finely chopped onion
40 g/1½ oz butter	3 tablespoons butter
25 g/1 oz flour	¼ cup all-purpose flour
300 ml/½ pint milk	1¼ cups milk
½ teaspoon mixed herbs	½ teaspoon mixed herbs
½ teaspoon salt	½ teaspoon salt
freshly ground pepper	freshly ground pepper
4-5 frankfurters, thinly sliced	4-5 frankfurters, thinly sliced
dried breadcrumbs	dried bread crumbs
butter	butter

Pull off all the skin from the roe (unless already processed) and mash the flesh with a fork. Fry the onion in the butter until light golden brown. Blend in the flour, add the milk gradually, stirring, and bring to the boil. Mix with the herbs and seasoning into the roe.

Place half the mixture in a deep ovenproof dish, dot all over with the sliced frankfurters, and cover with the rest of the roe. Sprinkle with the dried breadcrumbs, dot with flakes of butter and bake in a moderately hot oven (200°C, 400°F, Gas Mark 6) for 20-25 minutes until nicely browned.

Grilled Herring with Fennel
SERVES 4

METRIC/IMPERIAL	AMERICAN
4 (175-225-g/6-8-oz) herrings	4 (⅓-½-lb) herring
2 tablespoons chopped fresh fennel	3 tablespoons chopped fresh fennel
½ tablespoon salt	½ tablespoon salt
25 g/1 oz butter	2 tablespoons butter
1 teaspoon lemon juice	1 teaspoon lemon juice

Wash and scrub the fish well to remove all scales. Cut off the heads and trim the tails. Cut three narrow slits on the slant across each side. Mix the fennel and salt together and insert in the cuts and body cavity.

Melt the butter and lemon juice in a grill pan. Lay the fish in it and turn at once so the fish are coated all over. Grill under a hot grill for 4-5 minutes each side, basting once.

Variation: When fresh fennel is not available, use ¾ tablespoon dried fennel or dill seeds instead.

Stuffed Herrings
SERVES 4

METRIC/IMPERIAL	AMERICAN
4 large or 8 small herrings	4 large or 8 small herring
salt and pepper	salt and pepper
50 g/2 oz soft breadcrumbs	1 cup soft bread crumbs
25 g/1 oz chopped suet	3 tablespoons shredded suet
25 g/1 oz onion, finely chopped	¼ cup finely chopped onion
½ teaspoon mixed herbs	½ teaspoon mixed herbs
1 teaspoon chopped parsley	1 teaspoon chopped parsley
15-20 g/½-¾ oz walnuts, chopped	scant ¼ cup chopped walnuts
½ teaspoon salt	½ teaspoon salt
freshly ground black pepper	freshly ground black pepper
1 egg, beaten	1 egg, beaten
butter	butter

Scrub the herrings well to remove all the scales. Cut off the heads and tails. Split the fish down the belly from head to tail. Clean and carefully pull out backbones and as many of the small bones as possible. Lay the fish flat, flesh upwards, and season.

To make the stuffing, mix the rest of the dry ingredients together and bind lightly with the beaten egg. Spread evenly over the fish, roll up and tie with string. Pack the rolls into an ovenproof dish, dot with flakes of butter and bake in a moderately hot oven (190°C, 375°F, Gas Mark 5) for 25-30 minutes.

Serve with mustard dill sauce (see page 59), if liked.

Court Bouillon
MAKES 1.15 LITRES/2 PINTS (US 2½ PINTS)

Fish should never be boiled, hence the term 'poached'. In other words, the liquid should not be on a fast boil when the fish is lowered into it, and thereafter bubbles should hardly break the surface.

Poaching fish in court bouillon prior to serving with a sauce gives a far superior flavour to cooking in plain salted water.

If a fish kettle with its own strainer is not available, wrap the fish in muslin so it can be manoeuvred easily without danger of breaking.

Paella à la Valenciana (see page 61)
Overleaf: Turbot with Poppy Seed Rice (see page 62)

Fish suitable for poaching in court bouillon, whole or in cutlets or fillets, are: bass, cod, conger eel, flounder, haddock, hake, halibut, herring, jewfish, John Dory, mackerel, mullet, grey mullet, pike, skate (wings), sole and turbot.

METRIC/IMPERIAL	AMERICAN
1.15 litres/2 pints water	5 cups water
fish trimmings (tail, bones, skin, etc.)	fish trimmings (tail, bones, skin, etc.)
1 carrot	1 carrot
1 medium onion	1 medium onion
½ teaspoon salt	½ teaspoon salt
4-5 peppercorns, crushed	4-5 peppercorns, crushed
bouquet garni	bouquet garni
1 bay leaf	1 bay leaf
1 stick celery or ½ teaspoon celery seeds	1 stalk celery or ½ teaspoon celery seeds
1 tablespoon vinegar	1 tablespoon vinegar
2 tablespoons white wine	3 tablespoons white wine

Bring all the ingredients to the boil in a covered pan and boil for ½-1 hour. Strain before use. This stock will keep in a refrigerator for several days.

Baked Stuffed Pike (or Bass, Cod, Haddock)
SERVES 4

Any of these fish are good stuffed and baked in this manner.

METRIC/IMPERIAL	AMERICAN
1.25-1.5-kg/2½-3-lb fish	2½-3-lb fish
75 g/3 oz onion, very finely chopped	¾ cup very finely chopped onion
¾ tablespoon chopped capers	¾ tablespoon chopped capers
½ teaspoon chopped lemon (or common) thyme	½ teaspoon chopped lemon (or common) thyme
1 teaspoon dill weed	1 teaspoon dill weed
1 teaspoon salt	1 teaspoon salt
freshly ground black pepper	freshly ground black pepper
50 g/2 oz soft breadcrumbs	1 cup soft bread crumbs
75 g/3 oz butter, melted	6 tablespoons melted butter
1 small egg, beaten	1 small egg, beaten
dried breadcrumbs	dried bread crumbs
40 g/1½ oz butter	3 tablespoons butter
1½ tablespoons oil	2 tablespoons oil

Scrub the fish well to remove all the scales. Cut off gills and fins and trim the tail, but leave the head intact. Slit down the belly of the fish from head to tail and carefully cut out the backbone.

Make the stuffing: mix the onion, capers, herbs and seasoning with the breadcrumbs then stir in the melted butter. Stuff the fish with the mixture and sew up with a darning needle and thread. Brush all over with beaten egg, sprinkle with salt and pat on a coating of dried breadcrumbs. Melt the rest of the butter and the oil in a baking tin, lay the fish in it and baste well. Bake in a moderate oven (180°C, 350°F, Gas Mark 4), basting occasionally, for 40-45 minutes. Carefully turn the fish over once.

Serve with Tartare sauce (see page 86) or a piquant sauce if liked.

Grilled Mackerel with Mustard Dill Sauce
SERVES 4

METRIC/IMPERIAL	AMERICAN
4 (225-g/8-oz) mackerel	4 (½-lb) mackerel
salt	salt
50 g/2 oz butter	¼ cup butter
1 teaspoon lemon juice	1 teaspoon lemon juice
½ tablespoon dry mustard	½ tablespoon dry mustard
1 teaspoon anchovy essence	1 teaspoon anchovy extract
½ tablespoon vinegar	½ tablespoon vinegar
20 g/¾ oz flour	3 tablespoons all-purpose flour
250 ml/8 fl oz milk	1 cup milk
½ teaspoon chopped dill weed	½ teaspoon chopped dill weed

Wash thoroughly and clean the mackerel, remove the heads and trim the tails. Cut three narrow slits on the slant across each side. Sprinkle with salt.

Melt half the butter with the lemon juice in a grill pan. Lay the fish in it and turn at once so the fish are coated all over. Grill under a hot grill for 4-5 minutes each side, basting once.

Meanwhile make the sauce: stir the dry mustard into a paste with the anchovy essence and vinegar. In a small saucepan, melt the rest of the butter, blend in the flour, add the milk and stir with a wire whisk until it boils. Boil for 1-2 minutes then stir in the mustard mixture, dill weed and salt to taste. Bring again to the boil for serving.

Variation: The mackerel may be slit open and the bones removed before grilling. Grill flat, allowing 1-2 minutes less for each side.

Fish Salad
SERVES 4

Don't try this salad without the coriander!

METRIC/IMPERIAL	AMERICAN
675 g/1½ lb fillet of white fish (cod, haddock, etc.)	1½ lb fillet of white fish (cod, haddock, etc.)
6-8 spring onions, very finely chopped	6-8 scallions, very finely chopped
½ tablespoon ground coriander	½ tablespoon ground coriander
salt and pepper	salt and pepper
1 tablespoon tarragon vinegar	1 tablespoon tarragon vinegar
2-3 tablespoons wine vinegar	3-4 tablespoons wine vinegar

Wash the fish and drop it into gently boiling, salted water or court bouillon (see page 54). Simmer until cooked, about 12-16 minutes, depending upon the thickness of the fillet. Drain, remove skin and bones and flake the flesh.

Place a layer of fish in a decorative bowl, sprinkle with onion, coriander, salt and pepper. Repeat layers. Pour over the mixed vinegars and leave at room temperature for several hours before serving, or in a refrigerator until the following day.

59

Prawns à la Grecque (see page 60)

Cod Portugaise
SERVES 4

METRIC/IMPERIAL	AMERICAN
450 g/1 lb tomatoes	1 lb tomatoes
4 (225-g/8-oz) cod cutlets	4 (½-lb) cod cutlets
butter	butter
salt and pepper	salt and pepper
50-75 g/2-3 oz onion, finely chopped	½-¾ cup finely chopped onion
1 clove garlic, chopped and crushed (optional)	1 clove garlic, chopped and crushed (optional)
1 teaspoon chopped parsley	1 teaspoon chopped parsley
¼ teaspoon thyme	¼ teaspoon thyme
¼ teaspoon basil	¼ teaspoon basil
tarragon or wine vinegar	tarragon or wine vinegar
water	water
1 teaspoon sugar	1 teaspoon sugar

Skin and chop the tomatoes. Wash, trim and tie the cod cutlets into a neat shape. Place them in a buttered, shallow ovenproof dish and sprinkle with salt and pepper, the tomato, onion, garlic and herbs. Pour in equal quantities of vinegar and water to come halfway up the cutlets. Cover the dish with foil or greaseproof paper and bake in a moderate oven (180°C, 350°F, Gas Mark 4) for 30-35 minutes.

Pour off the liquid from the dish into a small saucepan. Stir in the sugar and, leaving the pan uncovered, boil rapidly to reduce by half. Serve the sauce separately.

Tulya
SERVES 4

METRIC/IMPERIAL	AMERICAN
450 g/1 lb fillet of white fish (cod, haddock, etc.)	1 lb fillet of white fish (cod, haddock, etc.)
juice of ½ small lemon	juice of ½ small lemon
salt	salt
225 g/8 oz potatoes	½ lb potatoes
3 rashers streaky bacon	3 slices bacon
1 tablespoon oil	1 tablespoon oil
1 medium onion, sliced	1 medium onion, sliced
1 tablespoon tomato purée	1 tablespoon tomato paste
300 ml/½ pint water	1¼ cups water
⅛ teaspoon cayenne pepper	⅛ teaspoon cayenne pepper
¼ teaspoon sugar	¼ teaspoon sugar
½ teaspoon basil	½ teaspoon basil

Cut the skin from the flesh of the fish and cut the flesh into large cubes; sprinkle with the lemon juice and salt to taste. Peel and cut the potatoes into rough 1-cm/½-inch cubes.

Cut the bacon into 2.5-cm/1-inch pieces and fry in the oil with the onion over moderate heat until the onion is soft and just beginning to colour. Pour in the tomato purée mixed with the water, cayenne and sugar.

Add the potato and basil, cover the pan and simmer for 20 minutes stirring occasionally, then add the fish and continue cooking for 10-15 minutes without stirring.

Shrimp à la Créole
SERVES 4

After a glorious swim in a Boston swimming pool, my friend's white-haired Negro butler served this dish under the trees. Nothing could have tasted better. It is almost as good indoors as out.

METRIC/IMPERIAL	AMERICAN
1 green pepper	1 green pepper
50 g/2 oz canned pimientos	2 oz canned pimientos
175 g/6 oz onions, coarsely chopped	1½ cups coarsely chopped onion
150-175 g/5-6 oz celery, finely sliced	⅓ lb celery, finely sliced
50 g/2 oz bacon fat or lard	¼ cup bacon drippings or lard
1 (793-g/1 lb 12-oz) can tomatoes	1 (1 lb 12-oz) can tomatoes
3 tablespoons tomato purée	4 tablespoons tomato paste
1 large clove garlic, finely chopped	1 large clove garlic, finely chopped
1 teaspoon paprika	1 teaspoon paprika
¼ teaspoon cayenne pepper	¼ teaspoon cayenne pepper
1 bay leaf	1 bay leaf
1 teaspoon salt	1 teaspoon salt
1½ teaspoons sugar	1½ teaspoons sugar
350 g/12 oz peeled fresh or frozen shrimps or prawns	1½ cups shelled fresh or frozen shrimp

Remove the stalk and seeds from the green pepper and chop the flesh into 1-cm/½-inch pieces. Chop the drained pimientos to about the same size.

Fry the green pepper, onion and celery in the fat until lightly coloured. Add the chopped tomatoes with their liquid and the rest of the ingredients, except the pimiento and shrimps or prawns. Cover the pan and simmer gently for 25-30 minutes until the vegetables are tender. Add the shrimps or prawns and pimiento and continue cooking for 5-7 minutes to heat through. Serve with boiled rice.

Prawns à la Grecque
SERVES 2

METRIC/IMPERIAL	AMERICAN
225 g/8 oz peeled fresh or frozen prawns	1 cup shelled fresh or frozen shrimp
50 g/2 oz butter	¼ cup butter
5 tablespoons chicken stock	6 tablespoons chicken stock
2 tablespoons lemon juice	3 tablespoons lemon juice
1 large clove garlic, chopped and crushed	1 large clove garlic, chopped and crushed
1 teaspoon chopped parsley	1 teaspoon chopped parsley
½ teaspoon thyme	½ teaspoon thyme
½ teaspoon dill weed	½ teaspoon dill weed
½ teaspoon ground coriander	½ teaspoon ground coriander
1½ tablespoons dry sherry	2 tablespoons dry sherry
salt and pepper	salt and pepper
1 tablespoon grated lemon rind	1 tablespoon grated lemon rind

Sauté the prawns gently in the butter for 3 minutes. Add the remaining ingredients except the sherry and continue cooking for 5-6 minutes. Remove from the heat, add the sherry and season to taste. Sprinkle with grated lemon rind and serve with plain boiled or pilau rice (see page 85).
(Illustrated on page 58.)

Prawn Curry

SERVES 4

Without the fresh spices and coconut milk with which this curry is made in India, it can be but a poor substitute here, but it is still very good.

Fresh coconuts can be bought at certain times of the year, and the grated flesh from one of these will give a far richer and fresher coconut milk than that made from desiccated coconut.

METRIC/IMPERIAL	AMERICAN
450 ml/¾ pint boiling water	2 cups boiling water
150 g/5 oz desiccated coconut	1⅔ cups shredded coconut
2 tablespoons ground coriander	3 tablespoons ground coriander
1 tablespoon ground cumin (jeera)	1 tablespoon ground cumin (jeera)
½ tablespoon ground turmeric	½ tablespoon ground turmeric
1½ teaspoons ground ginger	1½ teaspoons ground ginger
¾ teaspoon chilli powder (or a little less cayenne pepper)	¾ teaspoon chili powder (or a little less cayenne pepper)
1 teaspoon salt	1 teaspoon salt
2 tablespoons tamarind juice or vinegar	3 tablespoons tamarind juice or vinegar
1 large onion, finely sliced	1 large onion, finely sliced
2 large cloves garlic, crushed	2 large cloves garlic, crushed
3 tablespoons oil	4 tablespoons oil
450 g/1 lb peeled fresh or frozen prawns	2 cups shelled fresh or frozen shrimp

Pour the boiling water over the coconut and, when cool enough to handle, squeeze out as much milk as possible through a sieve. Make a paste of the spices and salt with the tamarind juice or vinegar.

In a flameproof casserole or frying pan, fry the onion in the oil until golden. Stir in the curry paste and garlic and continue frying, stirring continuously, for 3-4 minutes. Pour in the coconut milk and simmer, uncovered, for 10 minutes. Add the prawns, adjust seasoning and heat through.

Serve with boiled rice, allowing 350 g/12 oz (US 1¾ cups) long-grain rice, poppadums (to cook see page 63), Bombay duck (dried fish) and sambals (side dishes).

Paella à la Valenciana

SERVES 8-9

Paella is made with various ingredients combined with rice according to the region of Spain. The most colourful, and therefore the best known, is the combination which comes from Valencia.

A heavy copper omelette-shaped pan with two handles, called a 'sarten', is the traditional dish in which paella is cooked and served. If no sarten or frying pan large enough to take all the ingredients is available (it is not worth making a small quantity), the frying can be done in a frying pan and then the whole lot transferred to a casserole.

METRIC/IMPERIAL	AMERICAN
1.25 kg/2½-2¾ lb chicken	2½-2¾ lb chicken
1 pork fillet	1 pork tenderloin
2 calamari (cuttle-fish) or squid	2 calamari (cuttlefish) or squid
1 large green pepper	1 large green pepper
1 (113-g/4-oz) can pimientos	1 (4-oz) can pimientos
4-5 tablespoons olive oil	5-6 tablespoons olive oil
100 g/4 oz onions, finely chopped	1 cup finely chopped onion
2 cloves garlic, chopped and crushed	2 cloves garlic, chopped and crushed
2 tomatoes, skinned and chopped	2 tomatoes, skinned and chopped
350 g/12 oz long-grain rice	1½ cups long-grain rice
900 ml/1½ pints hot water	3¾ cups hot water
few strands of saffron	few strands of saffron
1 bay leaf	1 bay leaf
½ tablespoon salt	½ tablespoon salt
freshly ground black pepper	freshly ground black pepper
100 g/4 oz peeled fresh or frozen prawns	½ cup shelled fresh or frozen shrimp
100 g/4 oz black olives	¾ cup ripe olives
4 crawfish, cooked (optional)	4 crayfish, cooked (optional)
4 whole cooked prawns (Mediterranean if possible)	4 whole cooked Pacific prawns

Cut the chicken into small joints and the pork fillet into small cubes. Clean and slice the calamari. Discard stalk and seeds from the green pepper and cut the flesh of the pepper and the drained pimientos into strips.

Gently fry the chicken and pork in the oil until they are a light golden colour, add the calamari, onion and green pepper and continue frying for 3-4 minutes. Stir in the garlic, tomatoes and rice, add a little more oil if necessary, and fry for a further 3-4 minutes. Pour in the hot water with the saffron infused in it. Stir in the bay leaf, broken in half, with the salt, pepper, pimiento and prawns and allow to boil gently for about 20 minutes, or until the rice has absorbed all the liquid. Stir in the olives.

Serve with the chicken joints arranged on top and pieces of crawfish and whole prawns as garnish. *(Illustrated on page 55.)*

Gracie Fields' Fish Stew

SERVES 4

The inimitable Gracie Fields, the one and only 'Lancashire Lass', told me, 'No, no, I have never *thought* of dieting. I love food. Food — all of it.' Despite her restaurant in Capri, she loves the 'beautiful fish in England' and makes a bee-line for it whenever she visits her home country. This is one of her special recipes, which incorporates a cunning tang of ginger.

METRIC/IMPERIAL	AMERICAN
1 kg/2 lb halibut, turbot or hake, or 4 mackerel	2 lb halibut or hake, or 4 mackerel
1 medium onion, finely sliced	1 medium onion, finely sliced
1 teaspoon salt	1 teaspoon salt
$\frac{1}{8}$ teaspoon white pepper	$\frac{1}{8}$ teaspoon white pepper
$\frac{1}{2}$ tablespoon cornflour	$\frac{1}{2}$ tablespoon cornstarch
$\frac{1}{2}$ teaspoon ground ginger	$\frac{1}{2}$ teaspoon ground ginger
6 tablespoons lemon juice (from about 3 lemons)	$\frac{1}{2}$ cup lemon juice (from about 3 lemons)
2 eggs, beaten	2 eggs, beaten

Cut the fish into serving portions. Turn the onion into a large deep frying pan and cover with 1-2 cm/$\frac{1}{2}-\frac{3}{4}$ inch of water. Stir in salt and pepper, cover the pan, bring to the boil and boil for 3-4 minutes. Place the fish flat in the pan (the water should come halfway up the fish) and simmer, covered, for 10-15 minutes or until the fish is cooked. Remove the fish to a hot dish and, with a straining spoon, scatter the onions over the fish.

Make the cornflour and ginger into a paste with the lemon juice. Whisk in the beaten eggs, then 300 ml/$\frac{1}{2}$ pint (US $1\frac{1}{4}$ cups) of the strained fish liquor. Bring to the boil in a small saucepan, stirring all the time, and simmer for 2-3 minutes; adjust seasoning and pour over the fish.

Turbot with Poppy Seed Rice

SERVES 4

The crunch of the poppy seeds makes a good contrast to the fish in this dish.

METRIC/IMPERIAL	AMERICAN
1.25-1.5 kg/2$\frac{1}{2}$-3 lb turbot or halibut	2$\frac{1}{2}$-3 lb turbot or halibut
salt	salt
lemon juice	lemon juice
15 g/$\frac{1}{2}$ oz butter	1 tablespoon butter
50 g/2 oz onion, finely chopped	$\frac{1}{2}$ cup finely chopped onion
150 ml/$\frac{1}{4}$ pint white wine	$\frac{2}{3}$ cup white wine
$\frac{1}{4}$ teaspoon dill weed (optional)	$\frac{1}{4}$ teaspoon dill weed (optional)
lemon or white pepper	lemon or white pepper
1 teaspoon tomato purée	1 teaspoon tomato paste
3 tablespoons cream (optional)	4 tablespoons cream (optional)
100 g/4 oz peeled fresh or frozen prawns	$\frac{1}{4}$ lb shelled fresh or frozen shrimp
225 g/8 oz long-grain rice	1 cup long-grain rice
2 tablespoons poppy seeds	3 tablespoons poppy seeds

Remove the head and clean the fish. Cut across into four equal portions. Sprinkle with salt and lemon juice. Melt the butter in a large frying pan and gently fry the onion until slightly soft. Add the wine, dill weed and a good shaking of lemon or white pepper. Place the fish on top, cover the pan and simmer for 20 minutes.

Remove the fish to a hot dish. Add the tomato purée, cream and prawns to the frying pan and heat through. Test for seasoning and pour over the fish. Meanwhile cook the rice by your favourite method, strain and stir in the poppy seeds.
(Illustrated on pages 56-57.)

Note: If the poppy seeds are baked first in a moderately hot oven (190°C, 375°F, Gas Mark 5) for 5-8 minutes, it will bring out the nutty flavour and increase the crunchiness.

Kedgeree

SERVES 4

Although kedgeree is known as a breakfast dish, it is also delicious for supper and for parties. For these occasions thinly sliced onion, fried until brown and then dried, is particularly good scattered over the top. These dried onions can now be bought in packets, which saves a lot of trouble. The rice is also much more attractive if it is coloured in the Indian way with turmeric or saffron.

METRIC/IMPERIAL	AMERICAN
675 g/1$\frac{1}{2}$ lb smoked haddock, poached in milk and water	1$\frac{1}{2}$ lb smoked haddock, poached in milk and water
2-3 hard-boiled eggs	2-3 hard-cooked eggs
225 g/8 oz long-grain rice	1 cup long-grain rice
75-100 g/3-4 oz onions, finely chopped	$\frac{3}{4}$-1 cup finely chopped onion
100 g/4 oz butter	$\frac{1}{2}$ cup butter
$\frac{3}{4}$ teaspoon turmeric	$\frac{3}{4}$ teaspoon turmeric
1 bay leaf	1 bay leaf
salt and pepper	salt and pepper
chopped parsley	chopped parsley

Remove bones and skin from the haddock and flake the flesh roughly. Slice one egg and keep some aside for decoration. Chop the rest of the eggs. Drop the rice into boiling, salted water and boil until just tender, 12-14 minutes. Drain well.

Fry the onion gently in the butter for 3-4 minutes until soft but not coloured, add the turmeric and bay leaf and continue frying for a minute. Stir in the fish, then the rice and chopped egg and heat through over a gentle heat without stirring too much. Season with salt and pepper and turn out on to a hot dish.

Garnish with the reserved slices of hard-boiled egg, chopped parsley and dried fried onion if liked.

Note: The butter may be decreased and 1-2 tablespoons cream substituted, mixed in just before serving. This is especially good for serving as a breakfast dish.

Meat Dishes

Ceylon Beef Curry

SERVES 4

The national dish in Ceylon, as in India, is curry, but more often than not their curries include tomatoes, which grow in many parts of the island, and fresh coconut milk. If a fresh coconut is not available, make the milk from desiccated coconut as below.

METRIC/IMPERIAL	AMERICAN
675 g/1½ lb stewing steak	1½ lb beef stew meat
150 ml/¼ pint boiling water	⅔ cup boiling water
150 g/5 oz desiccated coconut	1⅔ cups shredded coconut
225-275 g/8-10 oz onions, finely chopped	2-2½ cups finely chopped onion
3 tablespoons vegetable fat or oil	¼ cup vegetable fat or oil
225 g/8 oz tomatoes, skinned and chopped	½ lb tomatoes, skinned and chopped
2-3 cloves garlic, finely chopped	2-3 cloves garlic, finely chopped
½ tablespoon ground coriander	½ tablespoon ground coriander
1½ teaspoons ground cumin (jeera)	1½ teaspoons ground cumin (jeera)
1 teaspoon ground cardamom	1 teaspoon ground cardamom
1 teaspoon ground turmeric	1 teaspoon ground turmeric
¼-½ teaspoon chilli powder (or cayenne pepper)	¼-½ teaspoon chilli powder (or cayenne pepper)
1 large potato, peeled and cubed (optional)	1 large potato, peeled and cubed (optional)
1½ teaspoons salt	1½ teaspoons salt
juice of ½ small lemon	juice of ½ small lemon

Remove any gristle from the meat and cut into 2.5-cm/1-inch cubes. Pour the boiling water over the coconut, leave to cool and then squeeze out as much of the liquid as possible; discard the coconut.

In a flameproof casserole fry the onion in the fat until golden brown. Stir in the tomatoes, garlic and spices and fry for 4-5 minutes. Add the meat and potato and continue frying until the red has disappeared. Stir in the coconut milk and salt, cover and simmer very gently for 1-1½ hours or until the meat is tender. Add a little water if the liquid evaporates too soon. Stir in the lemon juice a few minutes before the end of the cooking time.

Serve with boiled rice, allowing 350 g/12 oz (US 1½ cups) for 4, chutney, poppadums and sambals (side dishes).

To cook poppadums: Drop poppadums into 1 cm/½

inch of hot oil in a frying pan when they will swell immediately. After only a second or two, turn them over. Remove and drain.

Quick 'n Easy Beef Curry

SERVES 4

This curry can also be made with lamb if preferred.

METRIC/IMPERIAL	AMERICAN
675 g/1½ lb stewing beef	1½ lb beef stew meat
175-225 g/6-8 oz onion, sliced	⅓-½ lb onion, sliced
2 tablespoons oil	3 tablespoons oil
2 tablespoons curry powder	3 tablespoons curry powder
1 teaspoon ground cumin	1 teaspoon ground cumin
2 cloves garlic, chopped and crushed	2 cloves garlic, chopped and crushed
300 ml/½ pint beef stock (or water and 1 stock cube)	1¼ cups beef stock (or water and 1 bouillon cube)
50 g/2 oz sultanas	⅓ cup seedless white raisins
1 tablespoon chutney	1 tablespoon chutney
salt and pepper	salt and pepper

Remove gristle and any excess fat from the beef and cut the meat into convenient sized cubes. Fry the onion in the oil to a light brown, stir in the curry powder, cumin, garlic and meat and continue frying until all the red from the meat has disappeared, adding a little more oil if necessary. Stir in the stock, sultanas and chutney, cover and simmer for 45-60 minutes until the meat is tender. Adjust seasoning and add a little browning to give a good rich colour.

Serve with boiled rice, allowing 350 g/12 oz (US 1½ cups) raw long-grain rice, poppadums (see above) and sambals (side dishes).
(Illustrated on page 31.)

63

Chilita Beef Casserole

SERVES 4

Argentina — from which this recipe stems — exports some beautiful beef off the bone. Use any of their stewing cuts for this dish. If you choose home grown beef, I suggest chuck or top rump.

METRIC/IMPERIAL	AMERICAN
675 g/1½ lb chuck steak or top rump	1½ lb boneless chuck or rump steak
175 g/6 oz belly pork	⅓ lb pork picnic shoulder
1 tablespoon oil	1 tablespoon oil
225 g/8 oz onions, coarsely sliced	½ lb onions, coarsely sliced
½ beef stock cube	½ beef bouillon cube
1 (227-g/8-oz) can tomatoes	1 (8-oz) can tomatoes
1 (227-g/8-oz) can baked beans in tomato sauce	1 (8-oz) can baked beans in tomato sauce
1 teaspoon caraway seeds	1 teaspoon caraway seeds
½ teaspoon ground fenugreek	½ teaspoon ground fenugreek
½ teaspoon salt	½ teaspoon salt
freshly ground black pepper	freshly ground black pepper

Cut the beef into large cubes and the pork into 5 mm/¼ inch wide slices. Fry the pork in the oil until it begins to brown. Add the onion, cover the pan and cook over a medium heat for 5-7 minutes. Add the beef and fry gently, uncovered, until all the red has disappeared. Stir in the crumbled beef cube, turn into a casserole and add the rest of the ingredients. Cover and simmer gently in the oven for 2½-3 hours or until the beef is tender.

Chilli con Carne

SERVES 6

Chili seasoning is a blend of spices which is pungent rather than hot, and much used in Mexico. Chillies are small, very hot members of the capsicum family from which cayenne pepper is made.

For speed in cooking, two (283-g/10-oz) cans of kidney or red beans may be substituted for the dried beans. Simmer for 30-35 minutes only.

METRIC/IMPERIAL	AMERICAN
275 g/10 oz dried red beans	1½ cups dried kidney beans
1 large (150-175-g/5-6-oz) red or green pepper	1 large (5-6-oz) red or green pepper
100 g/4 oz onion, chopped	1 cup chopped onion
2 tablespoons oil	3 tablespoons oil
2-3 cloves garlic, chopped and crushed	2-3 cloves garlic, chopped and crushed
450 g/1 lb minced beef or lamb	1 lb ground beef or lamb
100 g/4 oz minced pork	½ cup minced pork
1 (396-g/14-oz) can tomatoes	1 (14-oz) can tomatoes
1 tablespoon chili seasoning	1 tablespoon chili seasoning
4 dried chillies, finely chopped	4 dried chilies, finely chopped
1½ teaspoons ground cumin	1½ teaspoons ground cumin
1 teaspoon oregano	1 teaspoon oregano
1½ teaspoons salt	1½ teaspoons salt

Wash the beans and soak in plenty of water overnight. Drain, reserving the liquid. Discard stalk and seeds from the pepper and chop the flesh roughly.

In a flameproof casserole (or fry in a frying pan and transfer to a casserole) fry the pepper and onion in the oil until the onion begins to colour, add the garlic and meat and continue frying until all the red from the meat has disappeared. Chop the tomatoes and stir in with the rest of the ingredients, adding 150 ml/ ¼ pint (US ⅔ cup) of the bean liquid. Bring to the boil and simmer, covered, on top of the cooker or in the oven, stirring occasionally, for 1½ hours or until the beans are just tender. A little more bean liquid may have to be added.

(Illustrated on pages 68-69.)

Steak à la Karlin

SERVES 4

Miriam Karlin is a comedienne-actress beloved by all because she is such fun offstage as well as on. She told me she thought she had one of the first auto-timed ovens in London. 'It's heaven for a working girl like me.' Her 'spiffing' party dish is this steak.

METRIC/IMPERIAL	AMERICAN
675-g/1½-lb piece rump or sirloin steak	1½-lb piece sirloin, rump or other good quality steak
2 tablespoons corn oil	3 tablespoons corn oil
150 ml/¼ pint red wine	⅔ cup red wine
1 tablespoon vinegar	1 tablespoon vinegar
¾ teaspoon chopped basil or mixed herbs	¾ teaspoon chopped basil or mixed herbs
salt and freshly ground black pepper	salt and freshly ground black pepper
225-350 g/8-12 oz tomatoes	½-¾ lb tomatoes
100 g/4 oz mushrooms	1 cup mushrooms
1 large or 2 small green peppers	1 large or 2 small green peppers
2 cloves garlic	2 cloves garlic
1 stick celery (optional)	1 stalk celery (optional)
25 g/1 oz flaked almonds, toasted	¼ cup toasted, slivered almonds

Marinate the meat in the oil, wine, vinegar, herbs and salt and pepper for several hours.

Skin and chop the tomatoes, wash and slice the mushrooms, deseed the pepper and slice the flesh, chop and crush the garlic and slice the celery, if used. Turn all the vegetables into a saucepan and sweat, covered, for 5 minutes, stirring occasionally.

Place the meat in a casserole and pour over the liquid in which it was marinated, the vegetables and the almonds. Season to taste. Cover and simmer in the oven for 1-1½ hours or until the steak is tender.

Place the steak on a hot dish and pour over the vegetable mixture. Slice to serve.

Grilled steak à la Bergman

Ingrid Bergman is one of the finest actresses and one of the most fascinating women that I have had the privilege of meeting. Over lunch we conversationally ranged the world, then settled on cooking, about which she had definite opinions. She and her family are mad about herbs, so here is her favourite recipe for steak. Rub seasoning and finely chopped fresh herbs – dill, basil, marjoram, thyme and savory – into the steak. Brush well with oil and grill both sides to your own taste of rare to well done, then sprinkle with lots more of the chopped herbs before serving.

Spiced Bacon

SERVES 6

METRIC/IMPERIAL	AMERICAN
1.75-kg/4-lb piece forehock or middle gammon	4-lb ham butt
600 ml/1 pint cider	2½ cups cider
600 ml/1 pint stock (or water and 1 stock cube)	2½ cups stock (or water and 1 bouillon cube)
100 g/4 oz prunes, soaked overnight	⅔ cup prunes, soaked overnight
4 cardamoms, crushed	4 cardamoms, crushed
4 cloves	4 cloves
piece dried ginger root, crushed or bruised	piece dried ginger root, crushed or bruised
1 bay leaf	1 bay leaf
1 teaspoon peppercorns, crushed	1 teaspoon peppercorns, crushed
cornflour (optional)	cornstarch (optional)

Soak the bacon joint overnight, or cover with cold water, bring to the boil and drain. Place in a large pan with the cider and stock, bring to the boil and skim. Add the drained prunes with the spices, bay leaf and peppercorns, cover and simmer for 1 hour 20 minutes, then add the dumplings and continue simmering, covered, for a further 20-25 minutes.

To thicken the cooking liquor slightly for gravy, allow 15 g/½ oz (US 2 tablespoons) cornflour per 450 ml/¾ pint (US 2 cups) liquor.

Dumplings

METRIC/IMPERIAL	AMERICAN
50 g/2 oz rolled oats	½ cup rolled oats
125 g/4½ oz self-raising flour	1 cup plus 2 tablespoons all-purpose flour sifted with 1½ teaspoons baking powder
50 g/2 oz shredded suet	½ cup chopped suet
¼ teaspoon salt	¼ teaspoon salt
¼ teaspoon ground ginger	¼ teaspoon ground ginger
1 egg, beaten	1 egg, beaten

Turn all the dry ingredients into a bowl and stir in sufficient beaten egg to give a soft dough. Roll into walnut sized balls.

Wendy's Baked Gammon

SERVES 6

The piquant and fascinating Wendy Craig, star of television and screen, hasn't much time for fancy cooking with a family as well as a career, so this is the glamorous dish she gives her guests 'which needs so little work, you see'.

METRIC/IMPERIAL	AMERICAN
1.5-1.75-kg/3-4-lb middle gammon or forehock	3-4-lb cured ham, with rind
½ bay leaf	½ bay leaf
4 peppercorns, crushed cloves	4 peppercorns, crushed cloves
1 (454-g/1-lb) can pineapple chunks	1 (1-lb) can pineapple chunks
100 g/4 oz brown sugar	½ cup brown sugar
miniature bottle of rum	miniature bottle of rum

Cover the gammon with unsalted water and bring to the boil. Skim well, add bay leaf and peppercorns, cover and simmer, allowing 15 minutes per 500 g/ 1 lb. Rip off the skin. Place in a roasting tin, score the fat into diamond shapes and stick a clove into the centre of each. Drain the pineapple chunks. Mix the juice with the sugar and rum and pour over the gammon.

Bake for 1 hour in a moderate oven (160°C, 325°F, Gas Mark 3), basting occasionally. Add the pineapple chunks for the last 10-15 minutes.

Birgit's Roast Pork

SERVES 6-8

This is a recipe given to me in Denmark, where they like to serve it with pickled cabbage and caramelised potatoes.

METRIC/IMPERIAL	AMERICAN
1.75-kg/4-lb loin of pork with crackling	4-lb loin of pork with crackling
salt	salt
peppercorns	peppercorns
cloves	cloves
bay leaves	bay leaves

Ask the butcher to score the fat in narrow ribs downwards and then across about 5 cm/2 inches apart. Rub well all over with salt, then stick alternately into the ribs of fat (in lines less than 2.5 cm/1 inch apart) the peppercorns, cloves and pieces of bay leaves.

Stand the joint on a grid in a baking tin containing 5 mm-1 cm/¼-½ inch of water and baste with the water frequently. Roast in a moderate oven (180°C, 350°F, Gas Mark 4) for 2½ hours, allowing 30 minutes per 500 g/1 lb plus 30 minutes over.

Pour off most of the fat and use the rest of the liquid for gravy.

Pot Roast Hand of Pork

SERVES 8-9

This is a very economical and delicious joint. It is not only cheap to buy but cheap to cook, as it requires only one ring or hot plate.

METRIC/IMPERIAL	AMERICAN
2-2.25-kg/4½-5-lb hand of pork	4½-5-lb Boston butt of pork
salt	salt
50 g/2 oz lard or dripping	¼ cup lard or meat drippings
sprig of rosemary	sprig of rosemary
1 bay leaf	1 bay leaf
675 g-1 kg/1½-2 lb peeled mixed vegetables (onion, carrot, turnip, celery, etc.), cut in large pieces	1½-2 lb peeled mixed vegetables (onion, carrot, turnip, celery, etc.), cut in large pieces

Ask the butcher to score the rind deeply in fine ribs. Rub salt well all over into the joint. Melt the lard in a large, strong-bottomed saucepan and brown the meat all over in it. Add the rosemary and bay leaf, cover and reduce the heat. Cook gently for 1½ hours, turning the joint over occasionally.

Lift out the joint, put in the prepared vegetables, season, replace the meat on top and continue cooking for 1 hour, or until the meat and vegetables are tender.

Serve the meat, vegetables and gravy separately. Carve the meat, slicing from each end.

Note: The rind or fat of this joint will be rather tough. If it is desired crisp, place the joint under a medium grill for about 10 minutes until the crackling is browned.

Pork Fillet with Wine Sauce

SERVES 4

METRIC/IMPERIAL	AMERICAN
100 g/4 oz large prunes	⅔ cup large prunes
300 ml/½ pint red wine	1¼ cups red wine
¼ teaspoon ground cinnamon	¼ teaspoon ground cinnamon
575-675 g/1¼-1½ lb pork fillet	1¼-1½ lb pork tenderloin
40 g/1½ oz flour	⅓ cup all-purpose flour
salt and freshly ground black pepper	salt and freshly ground black pepper
75 g/3 oz butter	⅓ cup butter
225 g/8 oz spaghetti	½ lb spaghetti
2 tablespoons chopped chives	3 tablespoons chopped chives
150 ml/5 fl oz double cream	⅔ cup whipping cream
lemon juice	lemon juice

Soak the prunes in the wine overnight, or for several hours at least, then simmer gently in the wine with the cinnamon until the prunes are tender. Trim the pork fillet of any fat and cut the meat into 1-cm/½-inch slices. Flatten the slices slightly. Toss in a bag with the flour, seasoned with salt and pepper, until well coated all over. Fry briskly in half the butter until browned on both sides. Pour off surplus butter and stir in the wine from the prunes. Cover and simmer very gently for 15 minutes.

Meanwhile cook the spaghetti in boiling salted water until just tender. Drain, return to the pan with the remaining half of the butter and half the chives and season with salt and pepper. Turn on to a hot dish and sprinkle with the rest of the chives.

Add the cream and prunes (halved and stoned if preferred) to the meat and heat through thoroughly without boiling. Season with salt, pepper and lemon juice. Serve separately or poured over the spaghetti. *(Illustrated on page 70.)*

T'ang Tsu' (Sweet-Sour) Pork

SERVES 6

The correct mushrooms for this dish would be the Chinese dried variety, soaked and cooked, but canned mushrooms may be used instead. Also green (fresh) ginger gives the best flavour, but if unavailable use ground ginger.

METRIC/IMPERIAL	AMERICAN
75-100g/3-4 oz green pepper	1 green pepper
1 (368-g/13-oz) can pineapple chunks or slices	1 (13-oz) can pineapple chunks or slices
1 (283-g/10-oz) can water chestnuts	1 (10-oz) can water chestnuts
3 gherkins	3 small sweet dill pickles
1 (396-g/14-oz) can tomatoes	1 (14-oz) can tomatoes
2½ tablespoons cornflour	3 tablespoons cornstarch
1½ teaspoons chopped green or ½ teaspoon ground ginger	1½ teaspoons chopped green or ½ teaspoon ground ginger
4 tablespoons soy sauce	⅓ cup soy sauce
4 tablespoons wine vinegar	⅓ cup wine vinegar
675 g/1½ lb cooked pork, cubed	1½ lb cooked pork, cubed
1 (212-g/7½-oz) can button or grilling mushrooms, drained	1 (7½-oz) can button or grilling mushrooms, drained
¼ teaspoon Ve-Tsin or monosodium glutamate	¼ teaspoon monosodium glutamate
salt (optional)	salt (optional)

Discard stalk and seeds from the pepper and cut the flesh into large cubes. Drain the pineapple, retaining the juice. If pineapple slices are used, cut into 1-2-cm/½-¾-inch pieces. Drain the water chestnuts and cut over half of them into thick slices. Cut the gherkins into julienne strips.

Strain the juice from the can of tomatoes into a large saucepan; blend with the cornflour, ginger, pineapple juice, soy sauce and vinegar and bring to the boil, stirring. Add the pork, tomatoes cut in half, sliced water chestnuts, green pepper, pineapple, mushrooms, gherkins and Ve-Tsin and simmer for 6-7 minutes until the pepper is just tender. Season if necessary with salt. Serve with long-grain rice cooked by your favourite method. *(Illustrated opposite.)*

66

T'ang Tsu' (Sweet-Sour) Pork (see above)
Overleaf: Chilli con Carne (see page 64)

Barbecued Pork Chops

SERVES 4

METRIC/IMPERIAL	AMERICAN
4 spare rib chops, or 675 g- 1 kg/1½-2 lb belly of pork, cut in pieces	4 spare rib pork chops
15 g/½ oz lard	1 tablespoon lard
5 tablespoons tomato ketchup	6 tablespoons tomato catsup
2 tablespoons vinegar	3 tablespoons vinegar
2 tablespoons tarragon vinegar	3 tablespoons tarragon vinegar
4 tablespoons water	⅓ cup water
½ tablespoon soy sauce	½ tablespoon soy sauce
15-25 g/½-1 oz onion, finely chopped	2 tablespoons finely chopped onion
½ teaspoon celery seeds	½ teaspoon celery seeds
1 bay leaf, crumbled	1 bay leaf, crumbled
½ teaspoon ground ginger	½ teaspoon ground ginger
25 g/1 oz seedless raisins	3 tablespoons seedless raisins

In a flameproof casserole (or in a frying pan then transfer to a casserole), gently brown the meat in the lard. Mix remaining ingredients and pour over the meat. Cover and simmer very gently for 1-1½ hours, or until the meat is tender.

Note: If belly pork is used, this dish is best made the day before serving and left in a cold place so the fat can be skimmed off easily.

Hot-Sweet Pork Chops

SERVES 2

METRIC/IMPERIAL	AMERICAN
2 pork chops	2 pork chops
salt	salt
¼ teaspoon ground ginger	¼ teaspoon ground ginger
¼ teaspoon curry powder	¼ teaspoon curry powder
2 teaspoons grated orange rind	2 teaspoons grated orange rind
2 teaspoons made mustard	2 teaspoons prepared mustard
1-2 teaspoons honey	1-2 teaspoons honey

Cut off the skin and any excess fat from the chops. Sprinkle both sides with salt.

Mix the dry spices together, then make into a paste with the orange rind, mustard and honey. Spread half over one side of both chops and grill under medium heat for 6-7 minutes. Turn the chops over, use the remaining paste and grill.

Dubonnet Terrine

SERVES 8

This meat loaf can be served hot with a coating of mashed potato, cold coated with potato mayonnaise, or unadorned and left in the terrine or turned out on to a plate.

METRIC/IMPERIAL	AMERICAN
100 g/4 oz streaky bacon rashers, finely cut	¼ lb bacon slices, finely cut
450 g/1 lb lean pork	1 lb lean pork
350 g/12 oz calf's or lamb's liver	¾ lb calf or lamb liver
225 g/8 oz onion, finely chopped	2 cups finely chopped onion
1 clove garlic, finely chopped and crushed	1 clove garlic, finely chopped and crushed
¾ teaspoon marjoram	¾ teaspoon marjoram
¾ teaspoon savory	¾ teaspoon savory
1½ teaspoons salt	1½ teaspoons salt
freshly ground black pepper	freshly ground black pepper
5 tablespoons Dubonnet	⅓ cup Dubonnet
4 bay leaves	4 bay leaves

Cut the rinds from the bacon and line a 1-kg/2-lb loaf tin, an 18-cm/7-inch cake tin or a 1.5-litre/2½-pint (US 3-pint) earthenware terrine with the rashers. Put the pork and liver through a coarse mincer (or ask the butcher to do it for you). Mix in thoroughly the onion, garlic, herbs, salt and a generous amount of black pepper. Stir in the Dubonnet and turn into the prepared tin. Smooth and place the bay leaves along the top. Cover with foil and bake in a moderate oven (180°C, 350°F, Gas Mark 4) for 2 hours.

To serve hot: Remove the meat to an ovenproof dish. Strain the liquid from the tin into a measuring jug and make up to 300 ml/1 pint (US 2½ cups) with water. Bring to the boil in a saucepan, remove from the heat and stir in a large (142-g/5-oz) packet of instant potato. Coat the loaf with it and decorate using a fork. Place in a hot oven (230°C, 450°F, Gas Mark 8) for 20-25 minutes until browned.

To serve cold: Pour away the liquid. Place a smaller tin with a weight on top of the meat and leave until cold before turning out. If coating with potato, make up a large (142-g/5-oz) packet of instant potato as instructed on the packet and leave to cool. Mix together 4 tablespoons (US 5 tablespoons) mayonnaise, 2 tablespoons (US 3 tablespoons) wine vinegar, 1 tablespoon boiling water and 1 tablespoon each chopped chives and parsley. Stir thoroughly into the potato and coat the loaf with the mixture. Garnish with watercress if liked.

Pork Fillet with Wine Sauce (see page 66)

Casserole de Foie

SERVES 4

The fabulous French singer Juliette Greco used to enjoy cooking when she had time. Why? 'Because I am a Frenchwoman and I think we are just born with a knowledge of how to cook – here', she said, pointing to her heart. She likes 'not simple' food, with vegetables such as onions, aubergines and tomatoes stewed to a pulp with herbs. She likes calf liver cooked this way.

METRIC/IMPERIAL	AMERICAN
350-450 g/12 oz-1 lb sliced calf's liver	$\frac{3}{4}$-1 lb sliced calf liver
2 medium onions, sliced lengthways	2 medium onions, sliced lengthwise
25 g/1 oz butter	2 tablespoons butter
1 tablespoon olive oil	1 tablespoon olive oil
150 ml/$\frac{1}{4}$ pint water	$\frac{2}{3}$ cup water
2 teaspoons fresh or 1 teaspoon dried tarragon	2 teaspoons fresh or 1 teaspoon dried tarragon
1 teaspoon thyme	1 teaspoon thyme
1 teaspoon salt	1 teaspoon salt
freshly ground black pepper	freshly ground black pepper

Cut away any gristle and skin from the liver. In a flameproof casserole fry the onions in the butter and oil slowly until golden. Add the liver and continue frying for 2-3 minutes each side. Stir in the water, chopped herbs and seasoning and simmer slowly for 50-60 minutes.

Cumberland Sausage Hotpot with Spiced Oranges

SERVES 4

METRIC/IMPERIAL	AMERICAN
450 g/1 lb red cabbage	1 lb red cabbage
450 g/1 lb Cumberland or pork sausages	1 lb Cumberland or pork sausages
100-175 g/4-6 oz onions, roughly chopped	$\frac{1}{4}$-$\frac{1}{3}$ lb onions roughly chopped
2 teaspoons juniper berries	2 teaspoons juniper berries
1 teaspoon salt	freshly ground black pepper
freshly ground black pepper	1$\frac{1}{4}$ cups dry cider
300 ml/$\frac{1}{2}$ pint dry cider	1 tablespoon wine vinegar
1 tablespoon wine vinegar	4 tablespoons red currant jelly
3 tablespoons redcurrant jelly	2 dessert apples
2 dessert apples	

Cut out the hard centre stem from the cabbage and shred the rest coarsely. Turn into a flameproof casserole or saucepan with the sausages, onion, juniper berries, salt and pepper.

Mix together the cider, vinegar and redcurrant jelly and pour into the casserole. Bring to simmering point and simmer gently, covered, for 1 hour. Add the apples, with cores removed and cut into thick slices, and continue simmering for a further 1 hour. Serve with spiced orange slices.

Spiced Orange Slices

METRIC/IMPERIAL	AMERICAN
2 oranges	2 oranges
6 tablespoons water	$\frac{1}{2}$ cup water
50 g/2 oz sugar	$\frac{1}{4}$ cup sugar
8 cloves	8 cloves
$\frac{1}{8}$ teaspoon ground cinnamon	$\frac{1}{8}$ teaspoon ground cinnamon

Cut peel and pith from the oranges and slice the flesh across the width. Bring the water, sugar and spices to the boil and boil for 3 minutes. Add the orange slices and simmer for 2-3 minutes. *(Illustrated on page 79.)*

Tripe de Manio

SERVES 4

Food is high on the list of priorities for well known radio personality Jack de Manio, but he never weighs anything. 'I throw in everything I think of and it usually tastes absolutely splendid.' For more conventional cooks I discovered the necessary weights!

METRIC/IMPERIAL	AMERICAN
575-675 g/1$\frac{1}{4}$-1$\frac{1}{2}$ lb prepared tripe	1$\frac{1}{4}$-1$\frac{1}{2}$ lb fresh prepared tripe
100 g/4 oz mushrooms	1 cup mushrooms
150-175 g/5-6 oz onion, coarsely chopped	1$\frac{1}{4}$-1$\frac{1}{2}$ cups coarsely chopped onion
1 clove garlic, finely chopped	1 clove garlic, finely chopped
2 tablespoons olive oil	3 tablespoons olive oil
450 g/1 lb tomatoes, skinned and chopped	1 lb tomatoes, skinned and chopped
1 teaspoon chopped parsley	1 teaspoon chopped parsley
$\frac{1}{2}$ teaspoon chopped marjoram	$\frac{1}{2}$ teaspoon chopped marjoram
$\frac{1}{2}$ teaspoon chopped basil	$\frac{1}{2}$ teaspoon chopped basil
150 ml/$\frac{1}{4}$ pint chicken stock	$\frac{2}{3}$ cup chicken stock
4 tablespoons white wine	5 tablespoons white wine
1 teaspoon salt	1 teaspoon salt
freshly ground black pepper	freshly ground black pepper

Blanch the tripe three or four times by boiling, draining it and renewing the water each time. Cut it into 2.5-cm/1-inch squares. Wash the mushrooms and slice thinly, including stalks.

Fry the onion and garlic in the oil until soft but not coloured. Add the tripe, tomatoes and herbs and fry gently for a few minutes. Transfer to a flameproof casserole or saucepan with the stock, wine and seasoning and allow to simmer gently for 1$\frac{1}{2}$-2 hours, according to the tripe used. Add the mushrooms after 1 hour.

Arind Lamb
SERVES 4-5

METRIC/IMPERIAL	AMERICAN
1-kg/2-lb piece shoulder lamb (after boning)	2-lb piece shoulder lamb (after boning)
225 g/8 oz onions, finely sliced	$\frac{1}{2}$ lb onions, finely sliced
3 tablespoons oil	$\frac{1}{4}$ cup oil
2 teaspoons ground turmeric	2 teaspoons ground turmeric
1 tablespoon ground ginger	1 tablespoon ground ginger
1$\frac{1}{2}$-2 tablespoons curry powder	2-3 tablespoons curry powder
$\frac{1}{2}$ teaspoon salt	$\frac{1}{2}$ teaspoon salt
300 ml/$\frac{1}{2}$ pint stock (or water and 1 stock cube)	1$\frac{1}{4}$ cups stock (or water and 1 bouillon cube)
175-225 g/6-8 oz cauliflower florets	$\frac{1}{3}$-$\frac{1}{2}$ lb cauliflower florets
100 g/4 oz French beans	$\frac{1}{4}$ lb French beans
150 ml/5 fl oz natural yogurt	$\frac{2}{3}$ cup plain yogurt
chopped parsley	chopped parsley

Trim the joint of excess fat and cut the meat into large cubes. Gently fry the onion in the oil until golden, stir in the spices (and crumbled stock cube if used), meat and salt and continue frying for 7-10 minutes. Stir in the stock (or water), cover and simmer gently for 30 minutes; add the vegetables and continue simmering for a further 15 minutes. Stir in the yogurt, adjust seasoning and heat through without boiling. Sprinkle with chopped parsley. Serve with boiled rice and poppadums (see page 63) if liked. *(Illustrated on page 31.)*

Roast Lamb with Rosemary
SERVES 4-6

METRIC/IMPERIAL	AMERICAN
1 leg of lamb	1 leg of lamb
2-3 cloves garlic, sliced	2-3 cloves garlic, sliced
sprigs of rosemary	sprigs of rosemary
salt	salt
dripping	drippings

With a sharp knife, make small incisions all over the joint. Push a sliver of garlic into each one and mark with small sprigs of rosemary. Sprinkle all over with salt.

Place a large sprig of rosemary on a trivet standing in a roasting tin containing melted dripping, place the joint on it and place another sprig of rosemary on top. Baste with the dripping and roast in a moderate oven (180°C, 350°F, Gas Mark 4), allowing 25 minutes per 500 g/1 lb plus 25 minutes over, or allow a little more time if the meat is preferred well done. Turn the joint over once and baste occasionally while roasting. Serve with minted new potatoes.

Lamb pilau
SERVES 4

This is an attractive dish for a buffet party because it can be heated through in the oven covered with foil. For a party increase the quantities as desired; chicken may be used in place of the lamb if preferred. Serve with pilau rice (see page 85).

METRIC/IMPERIAL	AMERICAN
675 g/1$\frac{1}{2}$ lb best and middle neck of lamb	1$\frac{1}{2}$ lb-rib roast of lamb, cut in joints
2 cardamoms	2 cardamoms
3 cloves	3 cloves
5 peppercorns	5 peppercorns
$\frac{1}{2}$ clove garlic	$\frac{1}{2}$ clove garlic
1 teaspoon salt	1 teaspoon salt
water	water

Cut the joints into cutlets and remove the outer skin. Turn into a saucepan with the rest of the ingredients and cover with water. Bring to the boil, skim and simmer, covered, for 1 hour. Strain; cool the stock then remove the solid fat from the top. Trim any excess fat from the meat then cut the meat from the bones into 2.5-cm/1-inch pieces.

Sausage Stuffed Breast of Lamb
SERVES 3-4

If given notice a butcher will bone the lamb for you. If not, it is not difficult to do it yourself at home.

METRIC/IMPERIAL	AMERICAN
1 large breast of lamb, boned	1 large breast of lamb, boned
salt and freshly ground black pepper	salt and freshly ground black pepper
225 g/8 oz sausagemeat	1 cup sausagemeat
3 tablespoons sage and onion stuffing mix	4 tablespoons sage and onion stuffing mix
1 clove garlic, chopped and crushed (optional)	1 clove garlic, chopped and crushed (optional)
2 teaspoons chopped fresh or dried rosemary	2 teaspoons chopped fresh or dried rosemary
2 teaspoons chopped fresh or 1 teaspoon dried mint	2 teaspoons chopped fresh or 1 teaspoon dried mint
dripping or oil	drippings or oil

Lay the lamb flat, meat side up, cut off excess fat and flatten the joint as much as possible. Sprinkle with salt and pepper. Mix the rest of the ingredients together, except the dripping, and spread evenly over the meat.

Roll up loosely, starting at the narrow end, and tie in two or three places. Place the roll on a trivet standing in a roasting tin, baste with melted dripping or oil and roast in a moderate oven (180°C, 350°F, Gas Mark 4), allowing 30 minutes per 500 g/1 lb plus 30 minutes over, turning the roll over once.

Poultry and Game

Chicken Korma

SERVES 4-5

Curry – in all its forms – is the national dish of India. There are literally hundreds of different kinds; Korma (a mild savoury curry) is typical of the north.

METRIC/IMPERIAL	AMERICAN
1.25-1.5-kg/2½-3-lb chicken (dressed weight)	2½-3-lb chicken (dressed weight)
600 ml/1 pint soured cream or yogurt (solid curds in India)	2½ cups sour cream or yogurt (solid curds in India)
juice of ½ lemon	juice of ½ lemon
1½ teaspoons salt	1½ teaspoons salt
¼ teaspoon black pepper	¼ teaspoon black pepper
40 g/1½ oz butter	3 tablespoons butter
1 tablespoon oil	1 tablespoon oil
1 medium onion, finely sliced	1 medium onion, finely sliced
2 cloves garlic, chopped and crushed	2 cloves garlic, chopped and crushed
¼ teaspoon ground cloves	¼ teaspoon ground cloves
1½ tablespoons ground coriander	1½ tablespoons ground coriander
1 tablespoon ground cardamom	1 tablespoon ground cardamom
1½ teaspoons finely chopped green (fresh) ginger, or ½ tablespoon ground ginger	1½ teaspoons finely chopped green (fresh) ginger, or ½ tablespoon ground ginger
40 g/1½ oz ground almonds	⅓ cup ground almonds
15 g/½ oz desiccated coconut	1 tablespoon shredded coconut

Cut the chicken into neat joints and marinate them for 1 hour or more in the soured cream or yogurt, lemon juice, salt and pepper.

Melt the butter and oil together and fry the onion and garlic in it to a light golden colour. Then add the spices, ground almonds and coconut and continue frying gently for 3-4 minutes. Turn into a casserole; add the chicken joints with the marinade. Cover and simmer very gently in the oven for 1-1½ hours until the chicken is tender. The gravy should be thick and should have no other liquid added to it. Serve with pilau rice (see page 85).

Sutherland Steamed Chicken

SERVES 4-5

The exquisite-voiced Joan Sutherland, who charms the world with her singing, charmed me with her natural love of food as well. 'I love to cook a simple dish which I can just pop on the stove all together and forget. But it must have lots of onion and herbs mixed in', she said. Here it is.

METRIC/IMPERIAL	AMERICAN
1.5-kg/3-lb chicken (dressed weight)	3-lb chicken (dressed weight)
salt and pepper	salt and pepper
½ teaspoon thyme	½ teaspoon thyme
½ teaspoon basil	½ teaspoon basil
½ teaspoon marjoram	½ teaspoon marjoram
1½ bay leaves	1½ bay leaves
1 large or 2 medium onions, sliced lengthways	1 large or 2 medium onions, sliced lengthwise
275 g/10 oz long-grain rice	1¼ cups long-grain rice

Rub the chicken all over with salt and pepper and place it in a steamer. Mix the herbs, onion and ½ tablespoon salt with the rice and pack around the chicken. Steam steadily for 1½ hours, or until the chicken is tender.

Bog Myrtle Chicken Casserole

SERVES 4

Bog myrtle is not sold commercially, but it can be dried easily at home. If using dried, decrease the quantity by nearly half.

METRIC/IMPERIAL	AMERICAN
1.25-kg/2½-lb chicken, cut into joints, or 4 pieces	2½-lb chicken, cut into joints, or 4 pieces
25 g/1 oz flour	¼ cup all-purpose flour
salt and pepper	salt and pepper
75-100 g/3-4 oz mushrooms	1 cup mushrooms
100 g/4 oz streaky bacon	6 slices bacon
100-175 g/4-6 oz onion, sliced lengthwise	¼-⅓ lb onion, sliced lengthwise
2 tablespoons oil	3 tablespoons oil
25 g/1 oz butter	2 tablespoons butter
1 teaspoon bog myrtle, finely chopped	1 teaspoon bog myrtle, finely chopped
450 ml/¾ pint chicken stock (or water and 1 stock cube) and white wine mixed	2 cups chicken stock (or water and 1 bouillon cube) and white wine mixed

Shake the chicken pieces in the flour seasoned with salt and pepper in a bag until well coated. Quickly wash and dry the mushrooms and slice thickly.

Cut the bacon into pieces and fry with the onion in the oil until lightly browned. Transfer to a casserole. Add the chicken to the pan with the butter and brown on both sides. Add to the casserole with the rest of the ingredients, including any remaining flour. Cover and simmer in the oven for 45 minutes or until the chicken is tender. Adjust seasoning before serving.

Poulet à l'Estragon
SERVES 4

Hardy Amies needs no introduction — men as well as women admire his unique styling in clothes. He prefers the simple English dishes such as cottage pie and fried fish for every day, but partywise his taste is for French food. 'I feel a bit cheaty about this. I don't create. I just add bits of something I think will be nice to a good standard recipe', he told me. So here is his party piece.

METRIC/IMPERIAL	AMERICAN
1.5-kg/3-lb roasting chicken (dressed weight)	3-lb roasting chicken (dressed weight)
butter	butter
1-2 tablespoons chopped fresh or half quantity dried tarragon	1-3 tablespoons chopped fresh or half quantity dried tarragon
1 clove garlic, chopped and crushed	1 clove garlic, chopped and crushed
rock salt	coarse salt
freshly ground black pepper	freshly ground black pepper
lemon juice	lemon juice
2 tablespoons brandy	3 tablespoons brandy

Wash and wipe the inside of the bird well. Mash together 50 g/2 oz (US $\frac{1}{4}$ cup) butter with the tarragon, garlic and salt and pepper to taste. Stuff into the bird. Rub softened butter all over the outside and season with salt, pepper and lemon juice.

Lay the bird on its side in a roasting tin and roast in a hot oven (230°C, 450°F, Gas Mark 8) for 30 minutes, turning once. Then turn it breast upwards and continue roasting in a moderate oven (180°C, 350°F, Gas Mark 4) for 30 minutes, basting with the butter melted from the bird. Pour away less than half the fat and pour the rest into a small saucepan with 300 ml/$\frac{1}{2}$ pint (US 1$\frac{1}{4}$ cups) stock made from the giblets. Do not thicken. Heat through for gravy.

Pour the warmed brandy over the chicken, set it alight and, when the flames have subsided, return to the oven for 5-10 minutes.

Cream Turkey Aline
SERVES 4

This is my mother's favourite way of finishing up the Christmas turkey.

METRIC/IMPERIAL	AMERICAN
350 g/12 oz cooked turkey or chicken	$\frac{3}{4}$ lb cooked turkey or chicken
50 g/2 oz onion, finely chopped	$\frac{1}{2}$ cup finely chopped onion
40 g/1$\frac{1}{2}$ oz poultry fat or butter	3 tablespoons poultry fat or butter
25 g/1 oz flour	$\frac{1}{4}$ cup all-purpose flour
$\frac{1}{2}$ teaspoon ground ginger	$\frac{1}{2}$ teaspoon ground ginger
1 teaspoon chopped oregano	1 teaspoon chopped oregano
450 ml/$\frac{3}{4}$ pint turkey or chicken stock or milk	2 cups turkey or chicken stock or milk
salt	salt
chopped parsley (optional)	chopped parsley (optional)

Slice the turkey (and use stuffing as well if there is any left) and lay in a shallow ovenproof dish. Cover with foil and very gently heat through in a cool oven (150°C, 300°F, Gas Mark 2). In a small thick-bottomed saucepan, fry the onion in the fat until golden. Blend in the flour, ginger and oregano until smooth. Pour in the stock or milk and bring to the boil, stirring with a wire whisk. Add salt to taste and boil for 2-3 minutes. Pour over the bird and serve sprinkled with chopped parsley, if liked, for colour.

Poultry with Cold Curry Sauce
SERVES 8, OR 4 AS MAIN DISH

This makes a very good dish for a buffet party. Lay largish pieces of bird on a flat dish and pour the sauce all over the centre but not to cover the bird completely. Garnish the dish with watercress.

METRIC/IMPERIAL	AMERICAN
450 g/1 lb flesh of roasted turkey or chicken (1.5-kg/3$\frac{1}{4}$-3$\frac{1}{2}$-lb chicken roasted=450 g/1 lb flesh)	1 lb flesh of roasted turkey or chicken (3$\frac{1}{4}$-3$\frac{1}{2}$-lb chicken roasted= 1 lb flesh)
1 small onion, finely sliced	1 small onion, finely sliced
25 g/1 oz poultry fat or butter	2 tablespoons poultry fat or butter
$\frac{1}{2}$ tablespoon curry powder	$\frac{1}{2}$ tablespoon curry powder
$\frac{1}{4}$ teaspoon turmeric	$\frac{1}{4}$ teaspoon turmeric
25 g/1 oz flour	$\frac{1}{4}$ cup all-purpose flour
450 ml/$\frac{3}{4}$ pint chicken stock, (or water and 1 stock cube)	2 cups chicken stock (or water and 1 bouillon cube)
1 tablespoon cranberry sauce or redcurrant jelly	1 tablespoon cranberry sauce or red currant jelly
150 ml/5 fl oz double, single or soured cream	$\frac{2}{3}$ cup whipping, coffee or sour cream

Arrange the poultry flesh on a plate. Fry the onion in the fat until soft and transparent. Add the curry powder and turmeric and continue frying for 3-4 minutes. Blend in the flour, then stir in the stock gradually and bring to the boil. Cover and simmer for 15-20 minutes. Remove from the heat, stir in the sauce or jelly and rub through a sieve. When cold stir in the cream. Pour over the poultry flesh.

Le Lapin aux Pruneaux

SERVES 4-5

This is a Belgian dish I learned from the proprietor of a hotel in Le Zoute, which is unhappily now no more.

METRIC/IMPERIAL	AMERICAN
1-kg/2-lb rabbit, cut into joints	2-lb rabbit, cut into joints
450 ml/¾ pint red wine	2 cups red wine
4 tablespoons wine vinegar	5 tablespoons wine vinegar
1 medium onion, sliced	1 medium onion, sliced
8 peppercorns	8 peppercorns
2 bay leaves	2 bay leaves
1 large sprig or 1 teaspoon dried thyme	1 large sprig or 1 teaspoon dried thyme
salt and freshly ground black pepper	salt and freshly ground black pepper
350 g/12 oz prunes	2 cups prunes
40 g/1½ oz flour	6 tablespoons all-purpose flour
40 g/1½ oz butter	3 tablespoons butter
1 tablespoon oil	1 tablespoon oil
300 ml/½ pint water	1¼ cups water
1 tablespoon gooseberry jam or redcurrant jelly	1 tablespoon gooseberry jam or red currant jelly

Marinate the rabbit for 12-24 hours in two-thirds of the wine, the vinegar, onion, peppercorns, bay leaves, thyme and ½ tablespoon salt. At the same time, soak the prunes in water.

Drain and dry the pieces of rabbit and shake them in a paper bag containing the flour, well seasoned with salt and pepper. Fry in the butter and oil until browned all over. Transfer to a casserole.

Add the drained, stoned and halved prunes and the marinade from the rabbit with the rest of the wine and the water. Season, cover tightly and simmer gently in the oven for 1¼-1½ hours, or until the rabbit is tender. Remove from the heat and stir in the jam or jelly.

Grouse Casserole with Juniper

SERVES 4

METRIC/IMPERIAL	AMERICAN
2 large or 4 small grouse	2 large or 4 small grouse
25 g/1 oz flour	¼ cup all-purpose flour
salt and freshly ground black pepper	salt and freshly ground black pepper
16-20 button onions	16-20 button onions
25 g/1 oz butter	2 tablespoons butter
1 tablespoon oil	1 tablespoon oil
150 ml/¼ pint red wine	⅔ cup red wine
300 ml/½ pint stock	1¼ cups stock
1 teaspoon chopped basil	1 teaspoon chopped basil
8 juniper berries	8 juniper berries
175 g/6 oz mushrooms	1½ cups mushrooms

Coat the grouse with the flour, seasoned with salt and pepper. In a flameproof casserole (or after frying transfer to a casserole) fry the grouse and onions in the butter and oil until browned all over. Blend in the remaining flour until smooth. Stir in the wine, stock, basil and crushed juniper berries (crush with the back of a spoon) and season with salt and black pepper.

Cover and simmer in a moderate oven (160°C, 325°F, Gas Mark 3) for 1-1¼ hours, or until the birds are nearly tender; turn the grouse over occasionally. Add the washed mushrooms, left whole if small or thickly sliced, and continue cooking for 20-30 minutes.

Unwinese Pigeon

SERVES 4

It is a treat to eat with 'Professor' Stanley Unwin — that master of scrambled English. 'The anticipation of coming to lunch has been giving me deep joy in the drooly of the saliva glades' was his greeting! And he went on to enjoy his 'stuffle-down with a controlled burpy paradole'. This was his 'stuffle-down'.

METRIC/IMPERIAL	AMERICAN
2 large or 4 small pigeons	2 large or 4 small pigeons
50 g/2 oz streaky bacon rashers	3 slices bacon
2 tablespoons corn oil	3 tablespoons corn oil
1 medium onion, sliced	1 medium onion, sliced
15 g/½ oz flour	2 tablespoons all-purpose flour
½ tablespoon tomato purée	½ tablespoon tomato paste
6 tablespoons game or chicken stock	½ cup game or chicken stock
150 ml/¼ pint red wine	⅔ cup red wine
¾ teaspoon chopped rosemary	¾ teaspoon chopped rosemary
½ teaspoon salt	½ teaspoon salt
freshly ground black pepper	freshly ground black pepper

Cut pigeons (if large) in half along the backbone and cut the bacon into 1-2-cm/½-¾-inch pieces. Fry the pigeons in the oil until lightly browned and transfer to a casserole. Fry the bacon and onion in the remaining oil until golden brown. Stir in the flour, tomato purée, liquids, rosemary and seasoning. Pour into the casserole, cover and simmer in the oven for 1½-2 hours, or until the pigeons are tender.

Game Puffs

SERVES 4

These small puffs are an attractive way of finishing up a little leftover game.

METRIC/IMPERIAL	AMERICAN
75 g/3 oz cooked game	scant ¼ lb cooked game
25 g/1 oz ham	2 tablespoons chopped ham
50 g/2 oz mushrooms	½ cup mushrooms
15 g/½ oz butter	1 tablespoon butter
15 g/½ oz flour	2 tablespoons all-purpose flour
150 ml/¼ pint game or chicken stock	⅔ cup game or chicken stock
¼ teaspoon ground mace	¼ teaspoon ground mace
⅛ teaspoon cayenne pepper	⅛ teaspoon cayenne pepper
salt and pepper	salt and pepper
225 g/8 oz puff or flaky pastry	½ lb puff paste

Chop the game and ham into small pieces. Wash the mushrooms quickly and chop finely.

Melt the butter and sauté the mushrooms in it for a minute or two, stir in the flour until well blended then add the stock and bring to the boil, stirring. Boil for 1-2 minutes, remove from the heat and stir in the spices and meats; season with salt and pepper. Allow to get cold.

Roll out the pastry thinly on a floured board and cut into 12 circles with a 9-cm/3½-inch pastry cutter. Place a tablespoon of the mixture on one half of each circle, brush round the edges with cold water, fold over to make half moons and seal the edges firmly. Leave for 30 minutes or so, then drop into hot deep fat (180-190°C/350-375°F) or fry in a frying pan until golden brown all over.

Aylesbury Game Pie

SERVES 10-12

This dish is traditionally eaten cold but is also extremely good served hot. In ancient recipes it was directed that the meat be placed 'in a large earthenware game pie-dish'. These dishes had special lids moulded to look like a pastry crust, and were brought to the table, thus entitling what is, in fact, a casserole to be termed a 'pie'.

METRIC/IMPERIAL	AMERICAN
1 hare	1 hare
1 kg/2 lb veal (or chicken or turkey meat)	2 lb veal (or chicken or turkey meat)
675 g/1½ lb sausagemeat	3 cups sausagemeat
1½ teaspoons thyme	1½ teaspoons thyme
½ teaspoon salt	½ teaspoon salt
freshly ground black pepper	freshly ground black pepper
2 bay leaves	2 bay leaves
225 g/8 oz ham or bacon	½ lb cured ham or Canadian style bacon
2 tablespoons brandy	3 tablespoons brandy
2 tablespoons water	3 tablespoons water

Remove all the flesh from the hare and cut it into pieces 2.5-5 cm/1-2 inches in length. Cut the veal, free from skin and bone, in the same manner. Chop the liver and kidneys of the hare fairly finely and mix into the sausagemeat with the thyme, salt and a generous amount of pepper.

Place a bay leaf at the bottom of a 3-litre/5-pint (US 6-pint) casserole, then spread in layers first the sausagemeat, then the hare and veal mixed, seasoning to taste and lastly the ham. Repeat layers. Place the second bay leaf on top, pour in the brandy and water and cover the casserole with a lid. Make a flour and water paste and stick it round the rim as a seal so no steam can escape. Place the casserole in a hot oven (220°C, 425°F, Gas Mark 7) for 30 minutes, then lower the heat and continue cooking in a cool to moderate oven (150-160°C, 300-325°F, Gas Mark 2-3) for a further 3 hours.

Avocado Bombay

SERVES 3 AS A MAIN COURSE
SERVES 4 AS A STARTER

An unusual way of using up those bits and bobs of left-over turkey or chicken.

Serve on a bed of rice (allow 150g/5 oz raw long-grain rice). Tomato rice is particularly good for colour contrast, or herb rice.

METRIC/IMPERIAL	AMERICAN
175-200 g/6-7 oz cooked turkey or chicken	6-7 oz cooked turkey or chicken
40 g/1½ oz onion, finely chopped	⅓ cup finely chopped onion
25 g/1 oz apple, after peeling and coring	1 oz apple, after peeling and coring
15 g/½ oz butter	1 tablespoon butter
½ teaspoon ground cumin	½ teaspoon ground cumin
2 teaspoons curry powder	2 teaspoons curry powder
1 (298-g/10½-oz) can condensed cream of chicken soup	1 (10½-oz) can condensed cream of chicken soup
2 avocados	2 avocados

Cut the poultry flesh into bite-sized pieces. Chop the apple finely and fry in a small saucepan with the chopped onion in the butter until amber coloured, stir in the spice and fry for 2-3 minutes. Add the soup, bring to the boil, remove from heat and stir in the chicken or turkey.

Meanwhile cut the avocados in half, discard the stones. Peel and slice the flesh into 5-mm/¼-inch thick slices. Place over the bed of cooked rice and pour over the sauce.

Serve sprinkled with chopped parsley if liked.

Devilled Turkey Legs

SERVES 2

My husband would never give the drumsticks to anyone from a roast turkey so that they could be devilled later. But now, happily, they can be bought separately, in which case cook first and be sure to thaw thoroughly before cooking if bought frozen.

METRIC/IMPERIAL	AMERICAN
1 teaspoon made English mustard	1 teaspoon made English mustard
1 teaspoon German or French mustard	1 teaspoon German or French mustard
2 teaspoons curry powder	2 teaspoons curry powder
½ teaspoon ground ginger	½ teaspoon ground ginger
¼ teaspoon salt	¼ teaspoon salt
40 g/1½ oz butter	3 tablespoons butter
2 cooked turkey drumsticks	2 cooked turkey drumsticks

Work the mustards and spices into the butter until thoroughly blended.

Score deep cuts in the turkey flesh and fill with the butter. Spread any remaining butter over the top and grill quickly for 5-7 minutes, turning frequently.

Vegetables

Fennel and Cucumber Salad
SERVES 4

Surround this salad with halved orange slices for serving with duck, goose or pork.

METRIC/IMPERIAL	AMERICAN
175-225 g/6-8 oz fennel root	approx. $\frac{1}{2}$ lb fennel root
7-8 radishes	7-8 radishes
100 g/4 oz cucumber, unpeeled	$\frac{1}{4}$ cucumber, unpeeled
1 tablespoon lemon juice	1 tablespoon lemon juice
2 tablespoons olive oil	3 tablespoons olive oil
salt and pepper	salt and pepper
$\frac{1}{2}$ teaspoon chopped fresh mint	$\frac{1}{2}$ teaspoon chopped fresh mint
chopped parsley or chives	chopped parsley or chives

Remove any discoloured pieces from the fennel. Wash all the vegetables well and dry them. Cut the fennel into narrow strips, the radishes into thin slices and the cucumber into small cubes. Turn into a bowl.

Beat the lemon juice and oil together. Season well with salt and pepper and stir in the mint. Pour over the vegetables and turn them in the dressing. Sprinkle with chopped parsley or chives to serve.

Carrot Salad
SERVES 4

METRIC/IMPERIAL	AMERICAN
350 g/12 oz young carrots	$\frac{3}{4}$ lb young carrots
10-12 spring onions	10-12 scallions
1 tablespoon vinegar	1 tablespoon vinegar
3 tablespoons olive or corn oil	4 tablespoons olive or corn oil
$\frac{1}{2}$ teaspoon salt	$\frac{1}{2}$ teaspoon salt
freshly ground black pepper	freshly ground black pepper
$\frac{1}{4}$ teaspoon sugar	$\frac{1}{4}$ teaspoon sugar
$\frac{1}{2}$ tablespoon chopped fresh burnet and dill mixed (or 1 teaspoon dried dill weed and savory mixed)	$\frac{1}{2}$ tablespoon chopped fresh burnet and dill mixed (or 1 teaspoon dried dill weed and savory mixed)
$\frac{1}{2}$ tablespoon chopped parsley	$\frac{1}{2}$ tablespoon chopped parsley

Peel the carrots and grate them on a grater. Slice the onions very finely. Beat the vinegar and oil together with the seasoning and herbs, except the parsley. Mix thoroughly with the carrot and onion and turn into a bowl. Sprinkle over the chopped parsley to serve.

Beetroot and Soured Cream Salad
SERVES 4

METRIC/IMPERIAL	AMERICAN
450 g/1 lb beetroot, cooked	1 lb cooked beets
1 tablespoon chopped chives	1 tablespoon chopped chives
$\frac{1}{2}$ tablespoon chopped fresh or half quantity dried tarragon or thyme	$\frac{1}{2}$ tablespoon chopped fresh or half quantity dried tarragon or thyme
150 ml/5 fl oz soured cream or yogurt	$\frac{2}{3}$ cup sour cream or yogurt
salt and pepper	salt and pepper

Peel the beetroot and cut into 1-cm/$\frac{1}{2}$-inch cubes. Stir the herbs into the soured cream and season generously with salt and pepper. Mix with the beetroot. Serve chilled.

Oriental Pasta Salad
SERVES 6

METRIC/IMPERIAL	AMERICAN
1 (241-g/8$\frac{1}{2}$-oz) can pineapple chunks	1 (8$\frac{1}{2}$-oz) can pineapple chunks
175 g/6 oz pasta shells or short-cut macaroni	1$\frac{1}{3}$ lb shell or other macaroni
$\frac{1}{2}$ small cucumber	$\frac{1}{2}$ small cucumber
2 carrots	2 carrots
225 g/8 oz fresh bean sprouts or 1 (283-g/10-oz) can	$\frac{1}{2}$ lb fresh bean sprouts or 1 (10-oz) can
4 spring onions	4 scallions
Dressing	**Dressing**
6 tablespoons salad oil	$\frac{1}{2}$ cup salad oil
3 tablespoons pineapple juice (from can)	$\frac{1}{4}$ cup pineapple juice (from can)
1 tablespoon wine vinegar	1 tablespoon wine vinegar
1$\frac{1}{2}$ tablespoons soy sauce	2 tablespoons soy sauce
$\frac{1}{2}$ teaspoon ground ginger	$\frac{1}{2}$ teaspoon ground ginger

Drain the pineapple, reserving the juice. Drop the pasta into boiling salted water and boil for 13-15 minutes until just tender. Drain. Meanwhile beat all the dressing ingredients together. Stir into the pasta while it is still warm to coat thoroughly. Allow to cool.

Slice the cucumber thinly and cut the peeled carrots lengthways, as thinly as possible. Mix with the bean sprouts and pineapple pieces into the pasta. Turn into a serving dish and garnish with spring onion lilies. Snip the green parts into small pieces and scatter them over the salad.

Cumberland Sausage Hotpot with Spiced Oranges (see page 72)
Overleaf: Sweet-Sour Stuffed Cabbage Leaves (see page 83)

Note: To make spring onion lilies, cut the onions 5 cm/2 inches from the bulb end then cut downwards several times with a sharp knife to within 5 mm/¼ inch of the bottom. Place in a bowl of cold water to open out.

Sweet-Sour Stuffed Cabbage Leaves

SERVES 6

This is a delicious variation on the Greek theme for stuffing cabbage leaves.

METRIC/IMPERIAL	AMERICAN
6 large green cabbage leaves	6 large green cabbage leaves
100 g/4 oz long-grain rice	½ cup long-grain rice
100-125 g/4½ oz onion, chopped	1 cup chopped onion
2 tablespoons oil	3 tablespoons oil
450 g/1 lb sausagemeat	2 cups sausagemeat
1½ teaspoons dried mixed herbs	1½ teaspoons dried mixed herbs
½ teaspoon caraway seeds	½ teaspoon caraway seeds
½ teaspoon salt	½ teaspoon salt

Drop the cabbage leaves into boiling salted water and boil for only 2-3 minutes. Drain and immediately plunge into cold water. Cut out the tough part of the spine from each leaf.

Cook the rice in boiling salted water until just tender. Drain. Fry the onion in the oil until light brown. Stir into the sausagemeat with the rice and the remaining ingredients. Divide into six portions.

Lay the leaves flat with the two sides of the 'V' (from the spines) overlapping. Press one portion of the meat mixture into the centre of each leaf and roll up, tucking in the ends to form neat 'packages'. Place closely together in a casserole or ovenproof dish, pour over the sauce, cover with a lid or foil and bake in a moderate oven (180°C, 350°F, Gas Mark 4) for 1 hour.

Sauce

METRIC/IMPERIAL	AMERICAN
50 g/2 oz onion, finely chopped	½ cup finely chopped onion
1 (396-g/14-oz) can tomatoes	1 (14-oz) can tomatoes
25 g/1 oz brown sugar	2 tablespoons brown sugar
2 tablespoons vinegar	3 tablespoons vinegar
1 medium carrot, grated	1 medium carrot, grated
50 g/2 oz seedless raisins	⅓ cup seedless raisins
salt and freshly ground black pepper	salt and freshly ground black pepper

Turn all the ingredients except seasoning into a pan, bring to the boil and boil for 5 minutes. Season to taste with salt and freshly ground black pepper.
(Illustrated on pages 80-81.)

Cabbage with Soured Cream

SERVES 4

METRIC/IMPERIAL	AMERICAN
675 g/1½ lb white cabbage	1½ lb white cabbage
40-50 g/1½-2 oz onion, finely chopped	approx. ½ cup finely chopped diced onion
150 ml/¼ pint water	⅔ cup water
½ teaspoon caraway seeds	½ teaspoon caraway seeds
1½ teaspoons salt	1½ teaspoons salt
freshly ground black pepper	freshly ground black pepper
1 tablespoon flour	1 tablespoon all-purpose flour
150 ml/5 fl oz soured cream	⅔ cup sour cream

Cut out the hard stalk from the cabbage and shred the leaves finely. Turn into a saucepan with the onion, water, caraway seeds and seasoning. Cover and boil for 5 minutes, stirring the cabbage once or twice.

Make a paste of the flour and the soured cream. Stir into the pan, bring again to the boil, stirring, and boil for 1-2 minutes.

Vegetable Stuffed Aubergines

SERVES 4

METRIC/IMPERIAL	AMERICAN
2 aubergines	2 eggplant
1 green pepper	1 green pepper
100 g/4 oz onion, chopped	1 cup chopped onion
100 g/4 oz celery, diced	1 cup diced celery
50 g/2 oz butter	¼ cup butter
100 g/4 oz long-grain rice	½ cup long-grain rice
225 g/8 oz tomatoes, skinned and chopped	½ lb tomatoes, skinned and chopped
1 chilli, seeded and chopped	1 chili, seeded and chopped
½ teaspoon salt	½ teaspoon salt
freshly ground black pepper	freshly ground black pepper
½ teaspoon basil	½ teaspoon basil
½ teaspoon tarragon	½ teaspoon tarragon
1 tablespoon Worcestershire sauce	1 tablespoon Worcestershire sauce
50-75 g/2-3 oz cheese, grated	½-¾ cup grated cheese

Cut the aubergines in half lengthways. Cut all round the insides, leaving a thick shell of the sides and base. Scoop out and chop the flesh. Remove the stalk and seeds from the pepper and chop the flesh roughly.

Fry the pepper, onion and celery in the butter until lightly browned, add the rice and continue frying for 3 minutes. Turn into a saucepan with the chopped aubergine and the rest of the ingredients, except the cheese, and cook gently, stirring frequently, for 8-10 minutes.

Fill the aubergine shells with this stuffing, mounding the tops, sprinkle liberally with cheese and bake in a moderately hot oven (190°C, 375°F, Gas Mark 5) for 40-45 minutes.
(Illustrated opposite.)

Vegetable Stuffed Aubergines (see above)

Rotkohl

SERVES 4-5

This is an Austrian recipe culled from a Viennese journalist friend.

METRIC/IMPERIAL	AMERICAN
675 g/1½ lb red cabbage	1½ lb red cabbage
1 medium cooking apple	1 medium baking apple
1 medium onion, thinly sliced	1 medium onion, thinly sliced
1 tablespoon brown sugar	1 tablespoon brown sugar
25 g/1 oz lard	2 tablespoons lard
150 ml/¼ pint red wine	⅔ cup red wine
4 tablespoons water	5 tablespoons water
1 teaspoon salt	1 teaspoon salt
freshly ground black pepper	freshly ground black pepper
½ teaspoon caraway seeds	½ teaspoon caraway seeds
3 cloves	3 cloves

Cut the cabbage into quarters and cut out the hard centre stalk. Shred finely. Peel, core and chop the apple coarsely.

Fry the onion and sugar in the lard until the onion is golden brown. Add the rest of the ingredients, cover and simmer for 40-45 minutes, stirring occasionally.

Sautéed Cucumber

SERVES 4

METRIC/IMPERIAL	AMERICAN
1 large cucumber	1 large cucumber
25 g/1·oz butter	2 tablespoons butter
salt	salt
grated nutmeg	grated nutmeg

Peel the cucumber and cut into 1-cm/½-inch dice. Sauté gently in the butter with the pan covered, stirring occasionally, until tender and lightly coloured, 8-10 minutes. Sprinkle with salt and nutmeg to serve.

Almonded Button Onions

SERVES 4

METRIC/IMPERIAL	AMERICAN
450 g/1 lb pickling onions	1 lb small onions
50 g/2 oz almonds, blanched and halved	½ cup blanched, halved almonds
40 g/1½ oz butter	3 tablespoons butter
1½ teaspoons brown sugar	1½ teaspoons brown sugar
½ teaspoon salt	½ teaspoon salt
⅛ teaspoon each cayenne pepper, grated nutmeg and ground cloves	⅛ teaspoon each cayenne pepper, grated nutmeg and ground cloves

Peel the onions carefully and leave whole. Fry the almonds very gently in the butter until they begin to turn golden, 1-2 minutes. Blend in the sugar, salt and spices, then add the onions and turn in the butter until well coated. Turn into a casserole, cover and bake in a moderate oven (180°C, 350°F, Gas Mark 4) for 25-30 minutes, until just tender.

Herbed Marrow with Green Pepper

SERVES 4

METRIC/IMPERIAL	AMERICAN
1-1.25 kg/2¼-2½ lb marrow	2¼-2½ lb summer squash
1 green pepper	1 green pepper
1 small onion, finely sliced	1 small onion, finely sliced
25 g/1 oz butter	2 tablespoons butter
1 teaspoon dill weed	1 teaspoon dill weed
¼-½ teaspoon mixed herbs	¼-½ teaspoon mixed herbs
¾ teaspoon minced garlic chips or 1 clove garlic, crushed	¾ teaspoon minced garlic chips or 1 clove garlic, crushed
1 teaspoon salt	1 teaspoon salt
freshly ground black pepper	freshly ground black pepper
4 tablespoons water	5 tablespoons water

Peel and cut the marrow into 2-cm/¾-inch cubes. Wash the pepper, discard stalk and seeds and slice the flesh coarsely.

In a flameproof casserole, fry the onion and pepper in the butter for 3-4 minutes until lightly softened. Add the herbs, garlic, salt and pepper to taste and sweat, covered, for 3-4 minutes. Stir in the marrow and water and simmer gently, covered, for 8-10 minutes or until the marrow is only just tender.

Broad Beans with Savory

SERVES 4

In France they boil every kind of green bean with sprigs of savory. For this I think winter savory is better, as it has a more pungent flavour to withstand the dilution by water. But for addition to a sauce, the more subtle flavour of summer savory is preferable.

METRIC/IMPERIAL	AMERICAN
1.25 kg/2½ lb broad beans (350-400 g/12-14 oz podded)	2½ lb lima or fava beans (12-14 oz podded)
15 g/½ oz butter	1 tablespoon butter
15 g/½ oz flour	2 tablespoons all-purpose flour
150 ml/¼ pint milk	⅔ cup milk
1 tablespoon chopped parsley	1 tablespoon chopped parsley
¾ teaspoon chopped fresh or half quantity dried summer savory	¾ teaspoon chopped fresh or half quantity dried summer savory
salt and pepper	salt and pepper

Drop the beans into boiling salted water and boil for 8-15 minutes (according to age), until tender. Drain.

Meanwhile make the sauce: melt the butter, blend in the flour, add the milk and bring to the boil, stirring with a wire whisk. Boil for 2-3 minutes, remove from the heat, add the herbs and season. Mix in the beans.

Potato Mint Casserole

This was a favourite dish of my husband's family and he always demands it as soon as the new potatoes make their appearance each spring!

The quantities must depend upon the appetite of the family. This dish can be served as a soup or it can form a main course.

Scrape small new potatoes and turn into a flame-proof casserole or saucepan. Cover with milk and season with salt and pepper. Add a large quantity of mint sprigs or leaves, enough to impregnate the milk and potatoes with the flavour. Bring to the boil and simmer gently for 15-20 minutes. Be careful that the milk does not overboil — it is best to keep the lid tipped up a little. Serve in soup bowls.

Pilau Rice
SERVES 4

To serve, mound the rice on a warm serving dish and stir in any meat used (see lamb pilau, page 73).

METRIC/IMPERIAL	AMERICAN
75 g/3 oz butter	6 tablespoons butter
1 tablespoon oil	1 tablespoon oil
50 g/2 oz onion, finely chopped	$\frac{1}{2}$ cup finely chopped onion
1 clove garlic, finely chopped	1 clove garlic, finely chopped
2.5-cm/1-inch stick cinnamon	1-inch stick cinnamon
4 cardamoms	4 cardamoms
3 cloves	3 cloves
1 bay leaf	1 bay leaf
350 g/12 oz long-grain rice	1$\frac{1}{2}$ cups long-grain rice
750 ml/1$\frac{1}{4}$ pints lamb stock	3 cups lamb stock
1$\frac{1}{2}$ teaspoons salt	1$\frac{1}{2}$ teaspoons salt
40-50 g/1$\frac{1}{2}$-2 oz blanched almonds or cashew nuts	$\frac{1}{3}$-$\frac{1}{2}$ cup blanched almonds or cashews
3 tablespoons sultanas	3 tablespoons seedless white raisins
2 small onions, finely sliced, or use bought crisp fried onion	2 small onions, finely sliced, or use bought crisp fried onion

In a flameproof casserole melt two-thirds of the butter with the oil and fry the chopped onion, garlic, cinnamon, cardamoms, cloves and bay leaf broken in half until the onion is soft but not coloured. Add the rice and continue frying for 3-4 minutes, stirring continuously. Pour in the stock and bring to the boil. Add the salt, cover the casserole with a piece of cloth then the lid and simmer very gently for 20-30 minutes, or until all the liquid is absorbed and the rice grains are separate.

Meanwhile fry the nuts and sultanas gently in the rest of the butter, stirring, until the nuts are a light golden colour. Remove and add the sliced onions to the pan (adding a little more fat if necessary) ; fry to a rich brown. Drain on kitchen paper.

As soon as the rice is cooked, gently stir in the nuts and sultanas with a fork, and sprinkle the fried onion over the top.

Yellow Rice
SERVES 4

This is an attractive way of serving rice either with a curry or with chicken, veal and fish dishes.

METRIC/IMPERIAL	AMERICAN
40 g/1$\frac{1}{2}$ oz butter	3 tablespoons butter
50 g/2 oz onion, finely chopped	$\frac{1}{2}$ cup finely chopped onion
$\frac{1}{2}$ teaspoon turmeric	$\frac{1}{2}$ teaspoon turmeric
225 g/8 oz long-grain rice	1 cup long-grain rice
600 ml/1 pint chicken stock	2$\frac{1}{2}$ cups chicken stock
$\frac{3}{4}$ teaspoon salt	$\frac{3}{4}$ teaspoon salt
2.5-cm/1-inch stick cinnamon, broken in half	1-inch stick cinnamon, broken in half
5 cardamoms	5 cardamoms
6 cloves	6 cloves

Melt the butter in a flameproof casserole or thick-bottomed saucepan and fry the onion gently until soft but not coloured. Blend in the turmeric then stir in the rice and fry slowly, stirring all the time, for 3-4 minutes. Add the stock, salt and spices and bring to the boil. Stir once, lower the heat to simmering, cover with a lid and allow to simmer for 15-17 minutes. Test the rice between the teeth; if not tender enough (it should still be a little firm in the centre) and the liquid is not completely absorbed, allow to cook longer. Turn into a bowl and fluff up with a fork.

Sauces and Accompaniments

Sauce Béarnaise

SERVES 3-4

METRIC/IMPERIAL	AMERICAN
$\frac{1}{2}$ teaspoon finely chopped shallot	$\frac{1}{2}$ teaspoon finely chopped shallot
$\frac{1}{2}$ teaspoon chopped tarragon	$\frac{1}{2}$ teaspoon chopped tarragon
1 teaspoon chopped chervil	1 teaspoon chopped chervil
$\frac{1}{2}$ teaspoon salt	$\frac{1}{2}$ teaspoon salt
freshly ground black pepper	freshly ground black pepper
$\frac{1}{8}$ teaspoon cayenne pepper	$\frac{1}{8}$ teaspoon cayenne pepper
2 tablespoons tarragon vinegar or 1 tablespoon and 1 tablespoon white wine	3 tablespoons tarragon vinegar or 1$\frac{1}{2}$ tablespoons and 1$\frac{1}{2}$ tablespoons white wine
2 large egg yolks	2 large egg yolks
75 g/3 oz butter	6 tablespoons butter

Turn the shallot, tarragon, chervil, seasoning and liquid into a small saucepan, bring to the boil and let it reduce by two-thirds. Remove from the heat and allow to cool a little. Stir in the egg yolks. Replace on a very gentle heat and beat in the butter, piece by piece, until the sauce is thick and smooth.

Cold Barbecue Sauce

SERVES 7-8

This cold barbecue sauce is especially good with grilled or fried fish, chicken, beefburgers or raw vegetables. It can also be served warm (but not hot) if preferred, and in a cold place or a refrigerator it will keep for many days.

METRIC/IMPERIAL	AMERICAN
150 ml/$\frac{1}{4}$ pint mayonnaise	$\frac{2}{3}$ cup mayonnaise
4 tablespoons tomato ketchup	5 tablespoons tomato catsup
1-2 teaspoons lemon juice (depending upon the mayonnaise)	1-2 teaspoons lemon juice (depending upon the mayonnaise)
1 teaspoon Worcestershire sauce	1 teaspoon Worcestershire sauce
1 teaspoon grated onion	1 teaspoon grated onion
1 teaspoon curry powder	1 teaspoon curry powder
$\frac{1}{2}$ teaspoon ground cumin	$\frac{1}{2}$ teaspoon ground cumin
$\frac{1}{4}$ teaspoon chilli powder or cayenne pepper	$\frac{1}{2}$ teaspoon chili powder or less cayenne pepper
1 teaspoon salt	1 teaspoon salt

Beat all the ingredients together thoroughly.

Tartare Sauce

SERVES 4

METRIC/IMPERIAL	AMERICAN
1 teaspoon finely chopped chives or onion	1 teaspoon finely chopped chives or onion
1$\frac{1}{2}$ teaspoons chopped capers	1$\frac{1}{2}$ teaspoons chopped capers
1$\frac{1}{2}$ teaspoons chopped gherkins	1$\frac{1}{2}$ teaspoons chopped sweet dill pickle
$\frac{1}{4}$ teaspoon chopped chervil	$\frac{1}{4}$ teaspoon chopped chervil
$\frac{1}{4}$ teaspoon chopped tarragon	$\frac{1}{4}$ teaspoon chopped tarragon
few drops of lemon juice	few drops of lemon juice
150 ml/$\frac{1}{4}$ pint mayonnaise	$\frac{2}{3}$ cup mayonnaise

Mix the first six ingredients into the mayonnaise.

Béchamel Sauce

MAKES 600 ML/1 PINT (US 2$\frac{1}{2}$ CUPS)

A real Béchamel sauce has infinitely more flavour than the butter, flour and milk concoction which often passes under the guise of Béchamel, but is in fact a plain 'white sauce'. Without the vegetables and spices, it cannot form a satisfactory substitute when true Béchamel is called for.

METRIC/IMPERIAL	AMERICAN
1 small onion, quartered	1 small onion, quartered
2 small carrots, chopped	2 small carrots, chopped
1 stick celery, chopped	1 stalk celery, chopped
$\frac{1}{2}$ bay leaf	$\frac{1}{2}$ bay leaf
2 cloves	2 cloves
4 peppercorns, slightly crushed	4 peppercorns, slightly crushed
$\frac{1}{8}$ teaspoon ground mace	$\frac{1}{8}$ teaspoon ground mace
1 teaspoon salt	1 teaspoon salt
600 ml/1 pint milk	2$\frac{1}{2}$ cups milk
40 g/1$\frac{1}{2}$ oz butter	3 tablespoons butter
40 g/1$\frac{1}{2}$ oz flour	6 tablespoons all-purpose flour
single cream (optional)	coffee cream (optional)

Bring the first eight ingredients and the milk to the boil. Remove from the heat, cover and allow to infuse for at least 30 minutes, then strain. Melt the butter, blend in the flour, add the strained milk and bring to the boil, stirring with a wire whisk. Boil for 1-2 minutes. A little cream may now be added if desired. Adjust seasoning and bring again to the boil.

Variation: (Quick method) If time does not permit preparation of the vegetables, a milder flavoured sauce can be made by sticking three cloves into a whole onion and standing the onion in the milk to infuse with the other seasonings. Then proceed as above.

Horseradish Sauce

MAKES 300 ML/½ PINT (US 1¼ CUPS)

This is a good accompaniment to roast or boiled beef, fried or grilled fish, and baked potatoes or beetroot.

METRIC/IMPERIAL	AMERICAN
1-2 tablespoons finely grated fresh horseradish or double quantity bottled horseradish cream	1-3 tablespoons finely grated fresh horseradish or double quantity bottled horseradish
300 ml/½ pint Béchamel sauce (see quick method, above)	1¼ cups Béchamel sauce (see quick method, above)
½ teaspoon lemon juice	½ teaspoon lemon juice
1-2 tablespoons single cream	1-3 tablespoons coffee cream
salt and pepper	salt and pepper

Mix horseradish into the Béchamel sauce to the strength you desire, add the lemon juice and cream and season fairly generously. Heat through.

Créole Sauce

SERVES 4-5

The original and perennial sarong girl, Dorothy Lamour, whose vital statistics have not changed since she first wowed the public in her sarong, gave me this recipe for her standby sauce. She usually makes about three times this quantity and keeps the rest in her freezer to use 'with chicken, veal, shellfish or anything. It's so handy when folk drop in,' she explained.

METRIC/IMPERIAL	AMERICAN
1 green pepper	1 green pepper
1 medium onion	1 medium onion
1 large clove garlic	1 large clove garlic
15 g/½ oz butter	1 tablespoon butter
½ tablespoon corn oil	½ tablespoon corn oil
1 (396-g/14-oz) can tomatoes	1 (14-oz) can tomatoes
1 tablespoon tomato purée	1 tablespoon tomato paste
1 bay leaf	1 bay leaf
½ teaspoon oregano	½ teaspoon oregano
¼ teaspoon thyme	¼ teaspoon thyme
½ teaspoon salt	½ teaspoon salt
freshly ground black pepper	freshly ground black pepper
1½ teaspoons sugar	1½ teaspoons sugar

Wash the pepper, discard the stalk and seeds and chop the flesh coarsely. Chop the onion to about the same size and the garlic very finely. In a large thick-bottomed saucepan, fry the onions in the butter and oil until golden. Add the pepper and garlic and continue frying for 4-5 minutes. Stir in the rest of the ingredients. Bring to the boil and simmer, covered, for 1¼-1½ hours, stirring occasionally.

Long Life Mint Sauce

MAKES 600 ML/1 PINT (US 2½ CUPS)

This sauce will keep indefinitely in a cupboard or dark place.

METRIC/IMPERIAL	AMERICAN
225 g/8 oz granulated sugar	1 cup sugar
600 ml/1 pint white malt vinegar	2½ cups white malt vinegar
100 g/4 oz chopped fresh mint (spearmint or apple mint)	¼ lb chopped fresh mint (spearmint or apple mint)

Bring the sugar and vinegar to the boil, stirring until the sugar is completely dissolved. Boil for 3 minutes then pour at once on to the mint. Leave, covered, until cold. Pour into (preferably) dark-coloured bottles.

Neapolitan Tomato Sauce

SERVES 3-4

A thick tomato sauce is particularly good with spaghetti, macaroni, tournedos or any meat requiring a piquant sauce.

METRIC/IMPERIAL	AMERICAN
1 large clove garlic	1 large clove garlic
4 tablespoons olive oil	5 tablespoons olive oil
1 onion, chopped	1 onion, chopped
2 tablespoons tomato purée	3 tablespoons tomato paste
2 tablespoons warm water	3 tablespoons warm water
1 (396-g/14-oz) can tomatoes	1 (14-oz) can tomatoes
½ small green pepper, chopped	½ small green pepper, chopped
½ teaspoon basil	½ teaspoon basil
½ teaspoon marjoram	½ teaspoon marjoram
small sprig of rosemary (optional)	small sprig of rosemary (optional)
1 bay leaf	1 bay leaf
½ teaspoon sugar	½ teaspoon sugar
½ teaspoon salt	½ teaspoon salt
freshly ground black pepper	freshly ground black pepper

Crush the clove of garlic without cutting it and heat in the oil without browning. Remove the garlic and sauté the chopped onion in the oil. Dilute the tomato purée with the warm water and add to the oil with the contents of the can of tomatoes (cut the tomatoes roughly, removing the cores) and the rest of the ingredients. Bring to the boil and simmer, uncovered, for 20-30 minutes, stirring occasionally. Remove the rosemary and bay leaf before serving.

Mint and Apple Jelly

MAKES 900 G/2 LB

For those who prefer a slightly sweeter mint accompaniment to their lamb than the traditional sharp mint sauce, this is a very popular jelly.

METRIC/IMPERIAL	AMERICAN
450 g/1 lb tart cooking apples (bramley seedlings are best)	1 lb baking apples
300 ml/½ pint malt vinegar	1¼ cups malt vinegar
450 g/1 lb granulated sugar	2 cups sugar
4 (well-packed) tablespoons chopped fresh mint	5 (well-packed) tablespoons chopped fresh mint
green food colouring (optional)	green food coloring (optional)

Wash and chop the unpeeled apples roughly, removing the seeds. Cover and boil with the vinegar until the apples are soft, about 10 minutes. Rub through a sieve. Return the pulp to the saucepan with the sugar, bring to the boil stirring, and boil fast for 7-9 minutes until a set is obtained. Remove from the heat and stir in the mint and a few drops of green food colouring, if desired. Pour into clean, warm, dry bottles and cover immediately.

Tarragon Vinegar

The best time to pick the leaves and make this vinegar — or any herb vinegar — is as soon as the flower buds appear on the plant but before they begin to open.

Pack a glass jar full of leaves. Fill the jar with white wine vinegar, cover and leave to infuse for 2 weeks. Strain and pour into bottles. A branch of tarragon put into each bottle makes it look glamorous and also increases the strength of the vinegar.

Variations: Any of the following vinegars — and any other you may like — can be made in exactly the same way: basil, burnet, marjoram, mint or mixed herb.

Herb and Spice Butters

This is a Danish idea made with their lovely creamy butter. Choose whichever flavour will complement the food you are serving.

For four people use half the normal 227-g/8-oz (US ½-lb) packet of butter, and cut into four equal pieces. Press each piece into any one of the following to coat all over, and serve as a garnish to hot food.

Orange Butter Serve with grilled fish, chops, bacon and gammon. Grate the zest of an orange on a medium grater, without scraping any of the pith beneath.

Nutty Butter Serve with grilled fish, lamb and pork chops. Chop salted peanuts finely.

Herb Butter Serve with grilled meat, fish, vegetables, pasta, rice, etc. Fresh chopped mixed herbs are infinitely superior to the dried varieties, but the dried can be used. A combination such as 'Herbes de Provence' gives a good flavour to pasta and rice especially.

Paprika Butter Serve with grilled chicken, rice and some vegetables.

Parsley and Lemon Butter Serve with grilled fish, beef, potatoes, chicory, etc. Grate the zest of a lemon on a medium grater and mix with chopped parsley.

Curry Butter Serve with grilled chicken, fish, potatoes, butter beans, etc.

Whipped Butter The Danes are also very fond of serving whipped butter with vegetables such as asparagus, artichokes, salsify, turnips, jacket potatoes, etc. Beat the butter with a hot wet spoon until light and fluffy and serve in a separate dish. *(Illustrated on pages 32-33.)*

Gooseberry Stuffing

MAKES SUFFICIENT FOR 1 DUCK

METRIC/IMPERIAL	AMERICAN
100-150 g/4-5 oz gooseberries	1½ cups gooseberries
1 duck liver	1 duck liver
25 g/1 oz butter	2 tablespoons butter
2½ teaspoons sage	2½ teaspoons sage
¾ teaspoon seasoned salt	¾ teaspoon seasoned salt
freshly ground black pepper	freshly ground black pepper
150 g/5 oz soft breadcrumbs	2½ cups soft bread crumbs

Wash, top and tail the gooseberries and chop them finely. Fry the liver in the butter for 2-3 minutes, then chop into small pieces. Mix the sage, salt and pepper into the breadcrumbs. Stir in the liver, the butter in which it was fried and the gooseberries. Mix well.

Sausage and Prune Stuffing

MAKES SUFFICIENT FOR A SMALL CHICKEN OR NECK OF 1 TURKEY

METRIC/IMPERIAL	AMERICAN
50 g/2 oz prunes	⅓ cup prunes
75 g/3 oz onion, finely chopped	¾ cup finely chopped onion
40 g/1½ oz butter	3 tablespoons butter
225 g/8 oz sausagemeat	1 cup sausagemeat
50 g/2 oz plain biscuit crumbs	¾ cup cracker crumbs
½ teaspoon dried mixed herbs	½ teaspoon dried mixed herbs
¼ teaspoon oregano	¼ teaspoon oregano
1 tablespoon sherry	1 tablespoon sherry
salt and pepper	salt and pepper

Pour boiling water over the prunes and leave them to

soak overnight. Drain, remove the stones and cut the flesh into small pieces.

Fry the onion in the butter until golden. Add the sausagemeat, biscuit crumbs and herbs and continue frying for 4-5 minutes. Remove from the heat, stir in the prunes and sherry and season with salt and pepper.

Pickled Onions
FILLS 2 (1-KG/2-LB) JARS

METRIC/IMPERIAL	AMERICAN
1 kg/2 lb pickling (silver-skin) onions	2 lb small onions
salt	salt
½ tablespoon mixed pickling spice	½ tablespoon mixed pickling spice
900 ml/1½ pints vinegar	3¾ cups vinegar
½ tablespoon sugar	½ tablespoon sugar

Sprinkle the peeled onions with salt and leave for several hours or overnight. Rinse off the salt and pat dry the onions. Pack tightly into two clean 1-kg/2-lb jam jars.

Bring the remaining ingredients to the boil, stirring until the sugar is dissolved, and boil for 5 minutes. Allow to cool, then strain over the onions. Cover when cold. Leave for 2-3 months before eating.

Pickled Eggs

Pickled eggs have been a favourite for snacks in old English country pubs for goodness knows how long, each landlord pickling them to his own recipe. I have been given recipes which vary from seven parts water to one part vinegar, to all vinegar. This is the strength I prefer, but try any variation to suit your own taste.

METRIC/IMPERIAL	AMERICAN
12 medium eggs	12 medium eggs
dried chillis	dried chili peppers
500 ml/17 fl oz water	generous 2 cups water
175 ml/6 fl oz white malt vinegar	¾ cup white malt vinegar
2 tablespoons whole pickling spice, tied in muslin	3 tablespoons whole pickling spice, tied in cheesecloth
5-cm/2-inch piece orange peel	2-inch piece orange peel
1 large clove garlic, halved	1 large clove garlic, halved

Bring the eggs to the boil in sufficient water to cover. Boil for 8-10 minutes, without the water boiling so furiously as to risk cracking the shells. Cool under a running cold tap to prevent a dark ring forming between the yolk and white. Shell carefully and pack into bottles. Place one chilli in each bottle.

Bring the rest of the ingredients to the boil and boil for 10 minutes. Allow to get cold. Strain over the eggs to cover them completely. Cover the bottles and leave for at least 1 month before serving.

Pickled Mushrooms
FILLS 2 (350-G/12-OZ) JARS

If too strong a flavour of vinegar is not appreciated; dilute the vinegar by substituting water for a quarter to half the amount.

METRIC/IMPERIAL	AMERICAN
450 g/1 lb button mushrooms	4 cups button mushrooms
white malt vinegar	white malt vinegar
2 blades of mace	2 blades of mace
4 peppercorns, lightly crushed	4 peppercorns, lightly crushed
1 teaspoon ground ginger	1 teaspoon ground ginger
1 teaspoon salt	1 teaspoon salt
15 g/½ oz onion, finely chopped	2 tablespoons finely chopped onion

Wash the mushrooms quickly, trim the stalks and cut any large mushrooms in half. Turn into a saucepan and just cover with vinegar. Stir in the rest of the ingredients. Bring to the boil, cover the pan and simmer very gently for 10-15 minutes.

Remove the mushrooms with a straining spoon and fill two (350-g/12-oz) jars. Strain over enough of the hot vinegar to cover, and seal the jars immediately. Leave for at least 2 weeks before opening.

Spiced Peaches
MAKES 1 KG/2 LB

These spiced peaches keep well and are delicious with gammon, bacon, other meats and poultry.

METRIC/IMPERIAL	AMERICAN
1 kg/2 lb peaches (unblemished)	2 lb peaches (unblemished)
675 g/1½ lb granulated sugar	3 cups sugar
450 ml/¾ pint cider vinegar	2 cups cider vinegar
175 ml/6 fl oz water	¾ cup water
2 teaspoons whole cloves	2 teaspoons whole cloves
2-4 sticks cinnamon	2-4 sticks cinnamon

Plunge the peaches into boiling water for a few seconds, then gently peel off the skins. Mix the sugar, vinegar, water and whole cloves together and boil, covered, for 5 minutes. Drop in the peaches, cover and simmer for 10-15 minutes until just tender. The time will depend upon the ripeness of the peaches.

Transfer to a sterilised wide-necked bottle or bottles (those with ground glass stoppers are best). Place sticks of cinnamon in each bottle and seal immediately.

(Illustrated on page 104.)

Suppers and Snacks

Caved Eggs
SERVES 4

METRIC/IMPERIAL	AMERICAN
4 crisp, round bread rolls	4 crisp, round bread rolls
$\frac{1}{2}$-$\frac{3}{4}$ tablespoon chopped fresh chives, savory and chervil or half quantity dried savory, chervil, basil or marjoram	$\frac{1}{2}$-$\frac{3}{4}$ tablespoon chopped fresh chives, savory and chervil or half quantity dried savory, chervil, basil or marjoram
100 g/4 oz cheese spread	$\frac{1}{2}$ cup cheese spread
salt and pepper	salt and pepper
4 eggs	4 eggs
butter	butter

Cut a slice off the bottom of each roll and scoop out all the soft crumbs inside. Work the herbs into the cheese spread and season with salt and pepper. Line the inside of each roll with the cheese. Break an egg into each, top with flakes of butter and bake in a moderately hot oven (190°C, 375°F, Gas Mark 5) for 14-16 minutes, until the eggs are set.

Guernsey Tomato and Mushroom Flan
SERVES 4

Grated cheese or chopped ham can be added as an exciting variation to this tasty light luncheon or supper dish.

METRIC/IMPERIAL	AMERICAN
450 g/1 lb tomatoes	1 lb tomatoes
100 g/4 oz mushrooms	1 cup mushrooms
1 small onion, finely sliced	1 small onion, finely sliced
25 g/1 oz butter	2 tablespoons butter
$\frac{1}{4}$ teaspoon basil	$\frac{1}{4}$ teaspoon basil
$\frac{1}{4}$ teaspoon savory	$\frac{1}{4}$ teaspoon savory
2 large eggs, beaten	2 large eggs, beaten
salt and pepper	salt and pepper
lightly baked 18-cm/ 7-inch flan case	lightly baked 7-inch pie shell
sprigs of parsley (optional)	sprigs of parsley (optional)

Skin the tomatoes by dropping them into boiling water for a few seconds then plunging them at once into cold water. Cut some into neat slices as garnish and keep aside. Chop the rest fairly finely. Wash the mushrooms quickly. Reserve one and cut the rest, unpeeled, into thick slices, including the stalks. Cut each slice into 2-3 pieces.

Fry the onion in the butter until golden. Add the mushrooms and continue cooking gently for 3-4 minutes. Remove from the heat and stir in the chopped tomato, herbs and well beaten eggs. Season well with salt and pepper and pour into the flan case.

Bake in a moderately hot oven (200°C, 400°F, Gas Mark 6) for 20 minutes then place the reserved mushroom in the centre and the tomato slices all around; continue baking for a further 15-20 minutes.

To serve, garnish with sprigs of parsley if liked.

Omelette aux Fines Herbes
SERVES 2

This is the favourite French omelette and really does require fresh herbs.

METRIC/IMPERIAL	AMERICAN
4 eggs	4 eggs
1-1$\frac{1}{2}$ tablespoons chopped fresh parsley, chives, chervil and tarragon mixed	1-2 tablespoons chopped fresh parsley, chives, chervil and tarragon mixed
salt and pepper	salt and pepper
15 g/$\frac{1}{2}$ oz butter	1 tablespoon butter

Break the eggs into a basin, add the herbs and a pinch of salt and pepper. Beat with a fork only long enough to blend the yolks and whites. Use an 18-cm/7-inch omelette pan and place it over a gentle heat to slowly become uniformly hot all over. Now add the butter. When it foams and begins to smoke slightly, but before it turns colour, pour in the eggs. Stir with a fork as if you were making scrambled eggs and, when they begin to set, lift the edges to allow any liquid still left to run underneath.

As soon as the mixture has set lightly but is still creamy on top, draw the pan away from the heat, tilt it away from you and fold the omelette over quickly (or roll it up). Turn out on to a hot plate and serve immediately. The whole process should not take more than 2-3 minutes. Lightly draw a piece of butter across the top to give it a glaze.

Sausage and Mushroom Minarets (see page 52)

Savoury Egg Pie

SERVES 4

METRIC/IMPERIAL	AMERICAN
225 g/8 oz shortcrust pastry (made with 225 g/ 8 oz flour)	basic pie dough (made with 2 cups all-purpose flour)
4 hard-boiled eggs	4 hard-cooked eggs
25 g/1 oz butter	2 tablespoons butter
25 g/1 oz flour	$\frac{1}{4}$ cup all-purpose flour
1$\frac{1}{2}$ teaspoons curry powder	1$\frac{1}{2}$ teaspoons curry powder
200 ml/7 fl oz milk	$\frac{3}{4}$ cup milk
1 tablespoon finely chopped pickle	1 tablespoon finely chopped relish
salt	salt

Roll out half the dough on a floured board and line an 18-cm/7-inch flan tin or ring with it.

Cut the eggs in half lengthways and lay them flat on the pastry, radiating from the centre. Melt the butter and blend in the flour and curry powder. Add the milk and stir with a wire whisk until it boils. Boil for 1-2 minutes, remove from the heat, and stir in the pickle, seasoning with salt as necessary. Pour over the eggs and leave until cold before covering.

Roll out the rest of the dough. Moisten the edge of the crust with cold water and cover the flan with the second piece, pressing the two edges together to stick firmly. Trim the edge and decorate the rim by marking with a knife handle. Prick the top with a fork, brush with milk and bake in a moderately hot oven (200°C, 400°F, Gas Mark 6) for 25-30 minutes, until nicely browned. Serve hot or cold.

Macaroni Cheese Special

SERVES 4-5

METRIC/IMPERIAL	AMERICAN
225 g/8 oz short-cut macaroni	2 cups macaroni
175 g/6 oz Cheddar cheese, cubed	1 cup cubed Cheddar cheese
25-40 g/1-1$\frac{1}{2}$ oz onion, very finely chopped	$\frac{1}{4}$-$\frac{1}{3}$ cup finely chopped onion
225 g/8 oz tomatoes, skinned and chopped	$\frac{1}{2}$ lb tomatoes, skinned and chopped
1 teaspoon basil or oregano	1 teaspoon basil or oregano
3 bacon rashers, chopped	3 bacon slices, chopped
25 g/1 oz butter	2 tablespoons butter
2 eggs	2 eggs
300 ml/$\frac{1}{2}$ pint milk	1$\frac{1}{4}$ cups milk
$\frac{1}{4}$-$\frac{1}{2}$ teaspoon paprika (optional)	$\frac{1}{4}$-$\frac{1}{2}$ teaspoon paprika (optional)
grated cheese	grated cheese
dried breadcrumbs	dried bread crumbs

Drop the macaroni into boiling, salted water and boil for 7-8 minutes until it is just tender; stir for the first 2-3 minutes to stop it sticking to the bottom. Drain.

In a casserole greased round the sides, place alternate layers of macaroni and the cubed cheese, onion, tomato, herb and bacon, finishing with macaroni. Dot each layer with flakes of butter. Beat the eggs with the milk and paprika, if used, and pour into the casserole. Sprinkle the top with grated cheese mixed with breadcrumbs, and bake in a moderate oven (180°C, 350°F, Gas Mark 4) for 40-45 minutes.

Spaghetti Caruso

SERVES 4

This is a dish Enrico Caruso, the great Italian tenor, enjoyed enormously and which has been named after him. He was a great gourmand so he probably liked far more spaghetti than the quantity given here. But this amount is usually ample for more ordinary appetites.

METRIC/IMPERIAL	AMERICAN
1 large red or green pepper	1 large red or green pepper
3 cloves garlic	3 cloves garlic
2 tablespoons olive oil	3 tablespoons olive oil
1 (396-g/14-oz) can tomatoes	1 (14-oz) can tomatoes
1 teaspoon chopped fresh or half quantity dried basil	1 teaspoon chopped fresh or half quantity dried basil
1 tablespoon chopped parsley	1 tablespoon chopped parsley
1$\frac{1}{2}$ teaspoons salt	1$\frac{1}{2}$ teapoons salt
freshly ground black pepper	freshly ground black pepper
$\frac{1}{4}$-$\frac{1}{2}$ teaspoon sugar	$\frac{1}{4}$-$\frac{1}{2}$ teaspoon sugar
225 g/8 oz courgettes	$\frac{1}{2}$ lb zucchini
40 g/1$\frac{1}{2}$ oz flour	6 tablespoons all-purpose flour
2 tablespoons olive oil	3 tablespoons olive oil
350 g/12 oz spaghetti	$\frac{3}{4}$ lb spaghetti
25-40 g/1-1$\frac{1}{2}$ oz butter	2-3 tablespoons butter
grated Parmesan cheese	grated Parmesan cheese

Remove the stalk and seeds from the pepper and cut the flesh into 5-mm/$\frac{1}{4}$-inch pieces. Cut the garlic into halves and, with a fork, squash round in the bottom of the pan in the oil while it is heating, then remove. Fry the pepper gently in the oil for 3-4 minutes, then add the tomatoes (removing the hard cores), herbs, seasoning and sugar. Cover the pan and allow to simmer for 15-20 minutes.

Slice the unpeeled courgettes to about 3 mm/$\frac{1}{8}$ inch thick. Shake the slices in a paper bag with the flour, seasoned with salt and pepper, until well coated. Shake off any surplus flour and fry in more oil until brown on both sides. Drain on absorbent paper.

Meanwhile cook the spaghetti: hold it in a bundle and lower the ends into boiling salted water in a large pan, then gradually wind the rest round the inside of the pan as it becomes supple enough to bend. Boil for 10-12 minutes until just tender (al dente). Drain, place in a pan in which you have melted the butter and toss until the spaghetti is coated. Turn the spaghetti on to a hot dish and pour over the sauce. Sprinkle lavishly with grated Parmesan and arrange the courgettes around the perimeter.

Karrysalat (see page 53)

Puddings and Sweets

Ginger Sponge Pudding

SERVES 4-5

METRIC/IMPERIAL	AMERICAN
75 g/3 oz butter	6 tablespoons butter
50 g/2 oz sugar	$\frac{1}{4}$ cup sugar
1 egg	1 egg
1$\frac{1}{2}$ tablespoons golden syrup	2 tablespoons corn or maple syrup
150 g/5 oz self-raising flour	1$\frac{1}{4}$ cups all-purpose flour, sifted with 1$\frac{1}{4}$ teaspoons baking powder
2 teaspoons ground ginger	2 teaspoons ground ginger
$\frac{1}{8}$ teaspoon salt	$\frac{1}{8}$ teaspoon salt

Beat the butter and sugar together until light coloured and fluffy. Beat in the egg, syrup and lastly the flour, sifted with the ginger and salt. Turn into a greased and floured 1-litre/2-pint (US 2$\frac{1}{2}$-pint) pudding basin. Cover with foil, twisting it under the rim (or use a basin with its own lid), and steam for 1$\frac{1}{2}$-1$\frac{3}{4}$ hours.

Serve with warm golden syrup diluted with a little water, if liked.

Summer Christmas Pudding

SERVES 5-6

This is a lovely Australian recipe and very appropriate, since the 25th of December is in the middle of the Australian summer. It makes a splendid party piece at any time of the year.

METRIC/IMPERIAL	AMERICAN
275 g/10 oz mixed dried fruit	scant 2 cups mixed dried fruit
1 teaspoon mixed spice	1 teaspoon mixed spice
$\frac{1}{4}$ teaspoon ground ginger	$\frac{1}{4}$ teaspoon ground ginger
$\frac{1}{4}$ teaspoon grated nutmeg	$\frac{1}{4}$ teaspoon grated nutmeg
50 g/2 oz sugar	$\frac{1}{4}$ cup sugar
1 tablespoon chocolate powder	1 tablespoon sweetened cocoa powder
450 ml/$\frac{3}{4}$ pint water	2 cups water
150 ml/$\frac{1}{4}$ pint bottled orange juice	$\frac{2}{3}$ cup bottled orange juice
15 g/$\frac{1}{2}$ oz gelatine	2 ($\frac{1}{4}$-oz) envelopes gelatin
75 g/3 oz chopped mixed peel	$\frac{1}{2}$ cup chopped candied peel
3 teaspoons sweet sherry	3 teaspoons sweet sherry
150-300 ml/5-10 fl oz double cream	$\frac{2}{3}$-1$\frac{1}{4}$ cups whipping cream
toasted almonds (optional)	toasted almonds (optional)

Turn the fruit with the spices, sugar and chocolate

powder into a saucepan with the water and orange juice. Bring to the boil and boil for 4-5 minutes until the fruit is soft and plump. Remove and stir in the gelatine (previously dissolved in a little very hot water). Mix in the chopped peel and the sherry and turn into a 19-cm/7$\frac{1}{2}$-inch ring mould rinsed out with cold water. Leave to set. Turn out and fill the centre hole with lightly whipped cream. Decorate all around with piped rosettes of cream with a toasted almond stuck into each, if desired, or decorate with sprigs of holly.

Variation: Use 300 ml/$\frac{1}{2}$ pint (US 1$\frac{1}{4}$ cups) Guinness in place of that amount of water and the sherry.

Steamed Date Pudding

SERVES 4-5

METRIC/IMPERIAL	AMERICAN
225 g/8 oz stoned dates	1$\frac{1}{4}$ cups pitted dates
50 g/2 oz self-raising flour	$\frac{1}{2}$ cup all-purpose flour, sifted with $\frac{1}{2}$ teaspoon baking powder
50 g/2 oz soft breadcrumbs	1 cup soft bread crumbs
50 g/2 oz soft brown sugar	$\frac{1}{4}$ cup (firmly packed) soft brown sugar
75 g/3 oz chopped suet	generous $\frac{1}{2}$ cup shredded suet
$\frac{1}{8}$ teaspoon salt	$\frac{1}{8}$ teaspoon salt
$\frac{1}{4}$ teaspoon ground ginger	$\frac{1}{4}$ teaspoon ground ginger
$\frac{1}{4}$ teaspoon ground cinnamon	$\frac{1}{4}$ teaspoon ground cinnamon
1 tablespoon brandy or sherry	1 tablespoon brandy or sherry
2 tablespoons milk	3 tablespoons milk
1 egg	1 egg

Chop the dates into fairly small pieces. Mix all the dry ingredients together. Beat the brandy or sherry and milk with the egg and stir into the dry ingredients. Turn into a greased and floured 1-litre/2-pint (US 2$\frac{1}{2}$-pint) pudding basin; tie down with greaseproof paper or twist foil under the rim. Steam for 2$\frac{1}{2}$ hours. Turn out on to a dish and serve with golden syrup, custard or cream, if liked.

Bilberry Pie

SERVES 4-5

METRIC/IMPERIAL	AMERICAN
225 g/8 oz rich shortcrust pastry (made with 225 g/8 oz flour and 1 egg yolk)	rich pie dough (made with 2 cups all-purpose flour and 1 egg yolk)
450 g/1 lb bilberries	4 cups blueberries
100-150 g/4-5 oz sugar	½ cup plus 2 tablespoons sugar
½ teaspoon ground cinnamon	½ teaspoon ground cinnamon
beaten egg or milk	beaten egg or milk
castor sugar (optional)	sugar (optional)

Roll out half the dough on a floured board and line a 20-23-cm/8-9-inch pie plate with it. Spread over the washed bilberries mixed with the sugar and cinnamon. Roll out the rest of the dough. Moisten the edges with cold water and place the second piece on top of the first, pressing the edges well together to stick firmly. Trim the edge. Brush the top with beaten egg or milk and sprinkle with castor sugar, if liked. Cut 3-4 slits to allow the steam to escape and bake in a moderately hot oven (200°C, 400°F, Gas Mark 6) for 25-30 minutes, until golden brown. Serve with cream or custard.

Date and Orange Flan

SERVES 4

METRIC/IMPERIAL	AMERICAN
175 g/6 oz stoned dates	1 cup pitted dates
4 tablespoons stout	5 tablespoons dark beer
¼ teaspoon ground cinnamon	¼ teaspoon ground cinnamon
¼ teaspoon ground cardamom	¼ teaspoon ground cardamom
2 oranges	2 oranges
baked 18-cm/7-inch flan case	baked 7-inch pie shell

Chop the dates roughly and boil with the stout and spices until it is the consistency of thick jam, 5-7 minutes. Grate the peel of one orange finely, reserving it for the syrup, and peel the other. Cut the flesh of both into thin slices and, with a pair of scissors, cut around each slice to remove all the pith.

Spread the date mixture in the flan case and arrange overlapping slices of orange in a circle on top. Pour over the syrup and allow it to set to form a glaze.

Syrup

METRIC/IMPERIAL	AMERICAN
1½ teaspoons arrowroot or cornflour	1½ teaspoons arrowroot or cornstarch
150 ml/¼ pint water	⅔ cup water
75 g/3 oz granulated sugar	6 tablespoons sugar
grated rind of 1 orange	grated rind of 1 orange

Make the arrowroot or cornflour into a smooth paste with a little of the water. Bring the rest of the water to the boil with the sugar and orange rind then stir and add the paste. Boil for 2-3 minutes until clear. Allow to cool before pouring over the flan.

Apple Charlotte

SERVES 4-5

METRIC/IMPERIAL	AMERICAN
675 g/1½ lb cooking apples, after peeling and coring	1½ lb baking apples, after peeling and coring
75 g/3 oz granulated sugar	6 tablespoons sugar
juice of ½ lemon	juice of ½ lemon
4 cloves	4 cloves
½ teaspoon ground cinnamon	½ teaspoon ground cinnamon
25 g/1 oz sultanas (optional)	2-3 tablespoons seedless white raisins (optional)
4 thin slices buttered bread from a large loaf	4 thin slices buttered bread from a large loaf
50 g/2 oz soft breadcrumbs	1 cup soft bread crumbs
soft brown sugar	soft brown sugar
butter	butter

Stew the apples with the granulated sugar, lemon juice, cloves, cinnamon and sultanas (if used) until the apples are soft and pulpy, 5-8 minutes. Roughly squash them with a fork.

Line the bottom and sides of a 1.5-litre/2¾-pint (US 3½-pint) pie dish with the bread slices, buttered side down. Pour the apple into the centre, scatter over the breadcrumbs and sprinkle thickly with soft brown sugar. Dot with flakes of butter and bake above centre in a hot oven (220-230°C, 425-450°F, Gas Mark 7-8) for 30-35 minutes, until the sugar has melted and the top is crunchy.

Flaming Apple Pancakes

SERVES 6

METRIC/IMPERIAL	AMERICAN
675 g/1½ lb cooking apples, after peeling and coring	1½ lb baking apples, after peeling and coring
1 tablespoon water	1 tablespoon water
175 g/6 oz granulated sugar	¾ cup sugar
½ teaspoon Angostura bitters	½ teaspoon Angostura bitters
¼ teaspoon ground cinnamon	¼ teaspoon ground cinnamon
pinch ground cloves	pinch ground cloves
6 pancakes (see page 96)	6 pancakes (see page 96)
25 g/1 oz almonds, cut into strips and toasted	3 tablespoons almonds, cut into strips and toasted
Calvados or brandy for flaming	Calvados or brandy for flaming

Slice or chop the apples roughly and bring to the boil with the water and sugar. Boil, stirring, until the apples are mushy. Remove from the heat and mash with a potato masher. Stir in the Angostura bitters and spices.

Spread each pancake with the apple mixture and roll up. Place in an omelette pan and heat over a spirit stove, or place in a shallow ovenproof dish and heat through in the oven. Scatter the almonds over the top, heat the Calvados or brandy and pour over the hot pancakes. Set alight and serve.

(Illustrated on pages 102-103.)

Spicy Cream Pancakes

MAKES 8

Pancakes can be made a day or two ahead and kept with pieces of foil or greaseproof paper between them, then all wrapped in paper, foil or a cloth. They keep best in a refrigerator.

METRIC/IMPERIAL	AMERICAN
100 g/4 oz plain flour	1 cup all-purpose flour
$\frac{1}{8}$ teaspoon salt	$\frac{1}{8}$ teaspoon salt
1 large or 2 small eggs	1 large or 2 small eggs
approx. 300 ml/$\frac{1}{2}$ pint milk and cold water, mixed	approx. 1$\frac{1}{4}$ cups milk and cold water, mixed

Filling	**Filling**
50 g/2 oz sultanas	$\frac{1}{3}$ cup seedless white raisins
2 tablespoons cream	3 tablespoons cream
40 g/1$\frac{1}{2}$ oz castor sugar	3 tablespoons sugar
$\frac{1}{2}$ teaspoon ground cinnamon	$\frac{1}{2}$ teaspoon ground cinnamon
225 g/8 oz curd cheese	1 cup curd cheese

Sift the flour and salt into a basin. Make a well in the centre and break in the eggs. Pour some of the liquid on and gradually stir in the flour by drawing it in from the sides. Whisk with a wire whisk, adding sufficient liquid to make the batter the consistency of thin cream. Leave aside for 30 minutes or more, then give it another whisk and turn into a jug (to make it easy for pouring).

To fry: Fry in oil (it simplifies the proceedings to have the oil in a jug as well). Pour in just enough oil to grease a small (15-18-cm/6-7-inch) frying pan. When it is hot, pour in just sufficient batter to thinly cover the bottom of the frying pan. Cook quickly until the underside is a pale golden brown, then lift with a spatula, adding a spot more oil. Turn the pancake over to cook on other side, or toss if preferred.

To fill: Soak the sultanas for an hour or so in warm water to plump them up, then drain.

Mix the cream, sugar and enough cinnamon into the cheese to give it a spicy flavour. Stir in sultanas and place spoonfuls of the filling along the centre of each pancake. Roll up, place in a shallow ovenproof dish, cover with foil and heat through gently in the oven. Sprinkle with more sugar and serve.

Vanilla Soufflé

SERVES 4

METRIC/IMPERIAL	AMERICAN
40 g /1$\frac{1}{2}$ oz butter	3 tablespoons butter
40 g/1$\frac{1}{2}$ oz plain flour	6 tablespoons all-purpose flour
225 ml/7$\frac{1}{2}$ fl oz milk, heated	1 cup milk, heated
50 g/2 oz vanilla sugar, or castor sugar and $\frac{1}{8}$ teaspoon vanilla essence	$\frac{1}{4}$ cup vanilla sugar, or superfine sugar and $\frac{1}{8}$ teaspoon vanilla extract
4 eggs	4 eggs
1 extra egg white	1 extra egg white

Melt two-thirds of the butter in a large saucepan. Blend in the flour and add the hot milk gradually, stirring with a wooden spoon until the mixture leaves the sides of the pan. Remove from the heat and beat in the sugar and the rest of the butter until perfectly smooth. Beat in the egg yolks one after the other.

Whip the egg whites stiffly and fold into the panada with a metal spoon. Turn at once into a greased and sugared 19-cm/7$\frac{1}{2}$-inch soufflé dish and bake in a moderate to moderately hot oven (180-190°C, 350-375°F, Gas Mark 4-5) for 25-30 minutes, until well risen and golden brown on top.

Variations: 1. Melt 50 g/2 oz (US 2 squares) plain chocolate in the milk before using it to make the panada.

2. Use half milk and half strong coffee.

3. Add 3 tablespoons (US $\frac{1}{4}$ cup) Grand Marnier to the panada. When serving the soufflé, pour a little Grand Marnier on to each plate. This causes the aroma to rise excitingly (a French tip!).

Melons Alaska

SERVES 4

The flavour of coriander makes this dish mysteriously intriguing. For anyone with a freezer or freezer compartment, an alternative to ice cream is a lemon sorbet — very refreshing on a warm evening.

METRIC/IMPERIAL	AMERICAN
2 Charentais or Ogen melons	2 Charentais, Ogen or similar melons
2 large egg whites	2 large egg whites
150 g/5 oz castor sugar	$\frac{1}{2}$ cup plus 2 tablespoons sugar
$\frac{1}{4}$-$\frac{1}{2}$ teaspoon ground coriander	$\frac{1}{4}$-$\frac{1}{2}$ teaspoon ground coriander
1 block chocolate and orange or vanilla ice cream	1 quart chocolate and orange or vanilla ice cream
2 tablespoons Grand Marnier or Curaçao	3 tablespoons Grand Marnier or Curaçao
32-36 halved, blanched almonds	32-36 halved, blanched almonds

Cut the melons in half horizontally and scoop out all the seeds. Whip the egg whites with a little of the sugar, adding the rest gradually with coriander to taste until stiff enough to stand up in peaks. Place a good portion of ice cream into the centre of each melon half and pour $\frac{1}{2}$ tablespoon or more of liqueur over each. Cover completely to the skin with the meringue, making sure there are no holes anywhere. Stick 8-9 almond halves into each and bake in a hot oven (230°C, 450°F, Gas Mark 8) for 3-4 minutes, until the meringue and almonds are lightly browned. Serve immediately.

Tiger Creams
SERVES 4

The quantities for this sweet will vary a little according to the size of the glasses used. Those given here will be sufficient for four reasonably large tall glasses.

METRIC/IMPERIAL	AMERICAN
250 ml/8 fl oz double cream	1 cup whipping cream
4 tablespoons milk	$\frac{1}{3}$ cup milk
6 tablespoons fine-cut (or chopped) marmalade	$\frac{1}{2}$ cup fine-cut (or chopped) marmalade
$\frac{1}{2}$ teaspoon ground cinnamon	$\frac{1}{2}$ teaspoon ground cinnamon
9 digestive biscuits, crushed	9 graham crackers, crushed

Reserving some of the cream for decoration, whip the cream and milk together until it will form soft peaks. Reserve sufficient marmalade for decoration, and mix the rest into the cream mixture. Stir the cinnamon into the biscuit crumbs until thoroughly mixed. Spoon into four tall glasses in alternating layers with the cream mixture and decorate as desired, either with piped cream and peel or blobs of marmalade.
(Illustrated on page 101.)

Stewed Plums
SERVES 4

Plums can be stewed more quickly in a saucepan on top of the cooker, but they tend to burst their skins and look untidy. The cinnamon is especially good with tart plums as it makes the flavour blander and smoother.

METRIC/IMPERIAL	AMERICAN
175 g/6 oz granulated sugar	$\frac{3}{4}$ cup sugar
$\frac{1}{2}$ teaspoon ground cinnamon	$\frac{1}{2}$ teaspoon ground cinnamon
4 tablespoons water	5 tablespoons water
675 g/1$\frac{1}{2}$ lb plums	1$\frac{1}{2}$ lb plums

Melt the sugar and cinnamon in the water in a covered casserole in the oven. Add the washed fruit and bake in a moderate oven (160-180°C, 325-350°F, Gas Mark 3-4) for 20-25 minutes, or until the plums are just tender, turning them over carefully once or twice.

Sagou à la Plaza
SERVES 4

I learned this simple sweet at one of the smartest hotels on the French Riviera, and it has been a favourite with my family ever since.

METRIC/IMPERIAL	AMERICAN
900 ml/1$\frac{1}{2}$ pints milk (some single cream makes it extra delicious)	3$\frac{3}{4}$ cups milk (some coffee cream makes it extra delicious)
1 vanilla pod	1 vanilla bean
50 g/2 oz sago	scant $\frac{1}{4}$ cup sago
50 g/2 oz castor sugar	$\frac{1}{4}$ cup sugar
1 egg yolk	1 egg yolk
4$\frac{1}{2}$ tablespoons double cream	5 tablespoons whipping cream
4 glacé cherries	4 candied cherries

Bring the milk to the boil with the vanilla pod in it. Scatter in the sago and boil, stirring, until every grain is transparent, 15-20 minutes. Remove from the heat and take out the vanilla pod. Beat in the sugar and egg yolk. Stir occasionally while it cools to prevent a skin forming, then pour into four glasses and chill.
    Decorate each glass with a rosette or blob of lightly whipped cream and a glacé cherry.

Variation: Chopped glacé fruit may be mixed into the sago after the sugar and egg yolk have been beaten in.

Floating Islands
SERVES 4-5

METRIC/IMPERIAL	AMERICAN
2 large eggs	2 large eggs
600 ml/1 pint milk	2$\frac{1}{2}$ cups milk
150 g/5 oz vanilla sugar, or castor sugar and vanilla essence	$\frac{1}{2}$ cup plus 2 tablespoons vanilla sugar, or superfine sugar and vanilla extract
glacé cherries and angelica	candied cherries and angelica

Separate yolks and whites of the eggs. Make a custard with the milk, egg yolks and 50 g/2 oz (US$\frac{1}{4}$ cup) of the sugar. Remove from the heat and, if plain sugar is used, add $\frac{1}{4}$ teaspoon vanilla essence or more to taste. Stir occasionally until cool to prevent a skin forming on the top. Pour into a large shallow dish.
    Whip the egg whites, adding the sugar gradually (with a little more vanilla essence if plain sugar is used) until stiff. Place in mounds on top of the custard. Chill.
    Decorate with chopped glacé cherries and angelica.

Variation: Turn the custard into a shallow ovenproof dish and put the mounds on top as above. Place in a very hot oven (240°C, 475°F, Gas Mark 9) for about 3 minutes until the 'islands' are lightly browned at the edges.

Breads, Biscuits and Cakes

Feather Gingerbread

This is intriguing because when the mixture is poured into the tin it is just like thick sauce. The result is a soft light cake which will keep in a cake box for at least 2 weeks without getting dry.

METRIC/IMPERIAL	AMERICAN
175 g/6 oz butter	$\frac{3}{4}$ cup butter
150 g/5 oz soft brown sugar	$\frac{1}{2}$ cup plus 2 tablespoons (firmly packed) soft brown sugar
225 g/8 oz black treacle	$\frac{2}{3}$ cup molasses
2 eggs, beaten	2 eggs, beaten
250 g/9 oz self-raising flour	$2\frac{1}{4}$ cups all-purpose flour, sifted with $2\frac{1}{2}$ teaspoons baking powder
$\frac{1}{2}$ teaspoon bicarbonate of soda	$\frac{1}{2}$ teaspoon baking soda
$\frac{1}{2}$ tablespoon ground ginger	$\frac{1}{2}$ tablespoon ground ginger
1 teaspoon ground cinnamon	1 teaspoon ground cinnamon
$\frac{1}{4}$ teaspoon ground cloves	$\frac{1}{4}$ teaspoon ground cloves
$\frac{1}{2}$ teaspoon grated nutmeg	$\frac{1}{2}$ teaspoon grated nutmeg
6 tablespoons Guinness or milk	$\frac{1}{2}$ cup dark beer or milk
6 tablespoons water	$\frac{1}{2}$ cup water
ginger butter icing (see below)	ginger butter icing (see below)
stem ginger	preserved ginger

Melt the butter and mix with the sugar and treacle. Stir in the beaten eggs until well blended. Sift the flour with the rest of the dry ingredients and beat into the butter mixture. Stir in the boiling Guinness and water and pour into an oiled and greaseproof-lined 29 x 23-cm/$11\frac{1}{2}$ x 9-inch roasting tin.

Bake in a moderate oven (180°C, 350°F, Gas Mark 4) for 40-45 minutes. Leave in the tin until cool before turning out on to a wire cake rack. Spread ginger butter icing over the top and smooth with a spatula or knife dipped in warm water.

Decorate with thin slices of stem ginger, arranged in the shape of a flower in the centre and petals at the corners. Sprinkle finely chopped ginger round the edge.

Ginger Butter Icing

METRIC/IMPERIAL	AMERICAN
100 g/4 oz butter	$\frac{1}{2}$ cup butter
225 g/8 oz icing sugar	2 cups sifted confectioners' sugar
1-2 tablespoons ginger syrup	1-3 tablespoons ginger syrup
ginger essence	ginger extract

Cream the butter well, add the sifted sugar and continue beating until the mixture is smooth and creamy. Gradually beat in ginger syrup and essence to give flavour and make the icing soft enough to spread.

Banana Bread

METRIC/IMPERIAL	AMERICAN
275 g/10 oz self-raising flour	$2\frac{1}{2}$ cups all-purpose flour, sifted with $2\frac{3}{4}$ teaspoons baking powder
$\frac{1}{2}$ teaspoon bicarbonate of soda	$\frac{1}{2}$ teaspoon baking soda
$\frac{1}{4}$ teaspoon salt	$\frac{1}{4}$ teaspoon salt
$\frac{1}{4}$ teaspoon ground cardamom	$\frac{1}{4}$ teaspoon ground cardamom
$\frac{1}{4}$ teaspoon ground mace	$\frac{1}{4}$ teaspoon ground mace
100 g/4 oz butter	$\frac{1}{2}$ cup butter
175 g/6 oz castor sugar	$\frac{3}{4}$ cup sugar
2 eggs	2 eggs
$\frac{1}{4}$ teaspoon vanilla essence	$\frac{1}{4}$ teaspoon vanilla extract
3 bananas, mashed	1 cup mashed banana
75 g/3 oz walnuts, chopped	$\frac{3}{4}$ cup chopped walnuts

Sift together the flour, bicarbonate of soda, salt and spices. Cream the butter and sugar until light and beat in the eggs and vanilla essence gradually. Stir in the flour and mashed banana alternately and lastly the nuts.

Turn into an oiled 1-kg/2-lb loaf tin, level the top and bake in a moderate oven (180°C, 350°F, Gas Mark 4) for 55-60 minutes. Leave in the tin to cool before turning out. Serve cut into slices and buttered.

Herb Bread

SERVES 4-5

This bread is delicious with many dishes for a party. The herbs can be varied to include parsley, chives, a little rosemary or lemon thyme. Parsley, chives and fennel or dill are good for serving with fish.

METRIC/IMPERIAL	AMERICAN
1 tablespoon (firmly packed) chopped fresh parsley, chives (plenty), marjoram, thyme and chervil	1 tablespoon (firmly packed) chopped fresh parsley, chives (plenty), marjoram, thyme and chervil
65 g/2½ oz salted butter	5 tablespoons salted butter
1 French loaf	1 French loaf

Mix the herbs thoroughly into the softened butter. Cut the loaf into diagonal 1-cm/½-inch slices, but not quite through, and spread each slice with some of the butter. Press the loaf together again and wrap in foil. Place in a hot oven (220°C, 425°F, Gas Mark 7) for 15-18 minutes.

Variation: For garlic bread, put 1-2 cloves of garlic through a garlic press, or chop finely and crush with a knife, then cream into the butter as above.

Speculaas

MAKES ABOUT 24

These are a special Dutch biscuit, always served on St. Nicholas Eve (5th of December) in Holland.

METRIC/IMPERIAL	AMERICAN
225 g/8 oz self-raising flour	2 cups all-purpose flour sifted with 2¼ teaspoons baking powder
⅛ teaspoon salt	⅛ teaspoon salt
1 teaspoon ground cinnamon	1 teaspoon ground cinnamon
½ teaspoon ground mixed spice	½ teaspoon ground mixed spice
175 g/6 oz butter	¾ cup butter
150 g/5 oz soft light brown sugar	½ cup plus 2 tablespoons (firmly packed) soft light brown sugar
grated rind of ½ lemon	grated rind of ½ lemon
100 g/4 oz ground almonds	1 cup ground almonds
25 g/1 oz shortbread biscuits, crushed	¼ cup crushed shortbread cookies
flaked almonds (optional)	flaked almonds (optional)

Sift the flour, salt and spices together. Cream the butter and sugar until light and fluffy. Beat in the lemon rind, then work in the ground almonds, biscuit crumbs and flour. Knead until smooth. Roll out on a floured board to less than 5 mm/¼ inch thick and cut into animal, little men or heart shapes, or into rounds with a 6-cm/2½-inch cutter. Flaked almonds may be scattered over the top and lightly pressed in, if liked. Bake on trays in a moderately hot oven (190°C, 375°F, Gas Mark 5) for 10-13 minutes until lightly coloured. Remove with a spatula and cool on a wire cake rack.

Ginger Shortbread Biscuits

MAKES ABOUT 30

These biscuits were my father's favourites, and he was seldom without some in stock. The amount of ginger can be varied according to the strength of the powder and individual taste.

METRIC/IMPERIAL	AMERICAN
32 g/1¼ oz ground ginger	1¼ oz ground ginger
350 g/12 oz plain flour	3 cups all-purpose flour
175 g/6 oz castor sugar	¾ cup sugar
250 g/9 oz butter	1 cup plus 2 tablespoons butter

Sift the ginger into the flour, stir in the sugar and rub in the butter. Knead until smooth.

Turn out on to a floured board and roll out to less than 5 mm/¼ inch thick. Cut into circles with a 5.5-cm/2¼-inch pastry cutter. Place on baking trays and bake in a moderately hot oven (190°C, 375°F, Gas Mark 5) until very lightly coloured, 25-30 minutes.

Poppy Seed Cocktailers

MAKES ABOUT 100

Little biscuits are ideal for serving with drinks of any kind. These will keep for weeks in an airtight container and indefinitely in a freezer.

METRIC/IMPERIAL	AMERICAN
75 g/3 oz poppy seeds	scant ½ cup poppy seeds
125 g/4½ oz plain flour	1 cup plus 2 tablespoons all-purpose flour
½ teaspoon salt	½ teaspoon salt
scant ⅛ teaspoon cayenne	scant ⅛ teaspoon cayenne
65 g/2½ oz butter and lard mixed	5 tablespoons butter and lard mixed
cold water	cold water

Turn the seeds on to a baking tray and bake in a moderately hot oven (200°C, 400°F, Gas Mark 6) for 15-20 minutes. Allow to get quite cold, then mix with all the dry ingredients in a bowl. Rub in the fats and stir in just sufficient cold water to bind the dough. Turn on to a floured board and roll out very thinly. Cut into circles with a 3.5-cm/1½-inch fluted pastry cutter. Place on baking trays and bake in the same moderately hot oven for 12-15 minutes, or until just before they turn brown. Sprinkle with salt before cooling, if liked.

Simnel Cake

A Simnel cake is most often served on Easter Sunday, but traditionally it should be made for Mothering Sunday.

METRIC/IMPERIAL	AMERICAN
225 g/8 oz butter	2 cups butter
225 g/8 oz castor sugar	1 cup sugar
3 large eggs	3 large eggs
275 g/10 oz plain flour	$2\frac{1}{2}$ cups all-purpose flour
$\frac{3}{4}$ teaspoon mixed spice	$\frac{3}{4}$ teaspoon mixed spice
$\frac{1}{2}$ teaspoon grated nutmeg	$\frac{1}{2}$ teaspoon grated nutmeg
$\frac{1}{4}$ teaspoon salt	$\frac{1}{4}$ teaspoon salt
225 g/8 oz currants	$1\frac{1}{3}$ cups currants
175 g/6 oz seedless raisins	1 cup seedless raisins
75 g/3 oz sultanas	$\frac{1}{2}$ cup seedless white raisins
100 g/4 oz chopped mixed peel	$\frac{2}{3}$ cup chopped candied peel
75 g/3 oz glacé cherries, halved (optional)	scant $\frac{1}{3}$ cup halved candied cherries (optional)
almond paste (see below)	almond paste (see below)
apricot jam	apricot jam

Cream the butter and sugar until light and fluffy. Beat in each egg separately. Sift all the dry ingredients together and stir into the creamed mixture. Add the fruit and turn half the mixture into an oiled and greaseproof-lined 20-cm/8-inch cake tin. Place a circle of almond paste on top, then cover with the rest of the cake mixture. Bake in a moderate oven (180°C, 350°F, Gas Mark 4) for 45 minutes, then lower the heat to 160°C, 325°F, Gas Mark 3, and continue baking for a further 2 hours. Leave in the tin until cool before turning out.

When quite cold, turn upside-down and spread lightly with sieved apricot jam. Cover the top with the second circle of almond paste, smooth it evenly and trim the sides. Roll the rest of the paste into 12 small balls (one for each of the Disciples) and place them around the outside edge. Brown lightly under the grill.

Almond Paste

METRIC/IMPERIAL	AMERICAN
350 g/12 oz ground almonds	3 cups ground almonds
175 g/6 oz castor sugar	$\frac{3}{4}$ cup sugar
175 g/6 oz icing sugar	$1\frac{1}{2}$ cups sifted confectioners' sugar
1 small egg and 1 egg yolk	1 small egg and 1 egg yolk
$\frac{1}{4}$ teaspoon almond essence	$\frac{1}{4}$ teaspoon almond extract

Mix together the almonds and sifted sugars. Make a well in the centre and add the lightly beaten egg and egg yolk with the almond essence, working into the dry ingredients and kneading thoroughly. Cut into three portions (two larger than the third). Roll out the larger pieces into 20-cm/8-inch circles, and use the rest for decoration.

100

Tiger Creams (see page 97)
Overleaf: Flaming Apple Pancakes (see page 95)

Drinks

Mint Tea

MAKES 4 CUPS

Peppermint or spearmint can be used for this tea. The former is said to be superior in flavour, but it depends upon individual taste.

The quantity of mint also depends upon the strength of flavour desired. I have given the quantity I prefer. Other herbs for tea may be treated in exactly the same way.

METRIC/IMPERIAL	AMERICAN
100-150 g/4-5 oz fresh mint, chopped or torn into little pieces (use more or less according to taste and time of year)	$\frac{1}{2}$-$\frac{2}{3}$ cup fresh mint, chopped or torn into little pieces (use more or less according to taste and time of year)
600 ml/1 pint boiling water	2$\frac{1}{2}$ cups boiling water
sugar or honey	sugar or honey

Turn the mint into a china or earthenware teapot. Pour over the boiling water and leave to infuse for 5 minutes. Strain to serve.

Sweeten with sugar or honey. A little lemon juice or a slice of lemon may also be added, if liked.

Mulled Ale

SERVES 3

Mulled ale was a very popular tipple in England in the 18th and 19th centuries and deserves a return to popularity. It is an excellent pick-you-up for invalids and influenza-weary patients, or anybody wanting a warm-up.

METRIC/IMPERIAL	AMERICAN
600 ml/1 pint (mild) ale	2$\frac{1}{2}$ cups beer
1 egg, beaten	1 egg, beaten
$\frac{1}{2}$ tablespoon sugar	$\frac{1}{2}$ tablespoon sugar
$\frac{1}{4}$ teaspoon ground mace	$\frac{1}{4}$ teaspoon ground mace
$\frac{1}{4}$ teaspoon grated nutmeg	$\frac{1}{4}$ teaspoon grated nutmeg

Stir 5 tablespoons (US 6 tablespoons) of the ale into the beaten egg. Bring the rest of the ale and the remaining ingredients to the boil, remove from the heat and allow to cool. Whip in the egg mixture and heat through *without* allowing it to boil (or the mixture will curdle).

Port Negus

SERVES 4-5

Florence Nightingale is said to have given Port Negus as a health-giving drink to the sick and wounded in the Crimea.

METRIC/IMPERIAL	AMERICAN
600 ml/1 pint port	2$\frac{1}{2}$ cups port
7.5-cm/3-inch stick cinnamon	3-inch stick cinnamon
$\frac{1}{4}$ teaspoon grated nutmeg	$\frac{1}{4}$ teaspoon grated nutmeg
$\frac{1}{2}$ tablespoon sugar	$\frac{1}{2}$ tablespoon sugar
150 ml/$\frac{1}{4}$ pint boiling water	$\frac{2}{3}$ cup boiling water

Heat the port with the cinnamon stick, nutmeg and sugar, but do not allow it to boil. Pour in the boiling water, remove the cinnamon and serve.

Burgundy Wine Cup

SERVES 10-12

This is a delicious cool drink for a summer's day.

METRIC/IMPERIAL	AMERICAN
2 bottles Burgundy	2 bottles Burgundy
300 ml/$\frac{1}{2}$ pint dry sherry	1$\frac{1}{4}$ cups dry sherry
150 ml/$\frac{1}{4}$ pint Chartreuse, Cointreau or Curaçao (optional)	$\frac{2}{3}$ cup Chartreuse, Cointreau or Curaçao (optional)
juice of 3-4 oranges or 175-200 ml/6-7 fl oz bottled orange, strained	juice of 3-4 oranges or $\frac{2}{3}$-1 cup concentrated orange drink, strained
juice of 2 lemons	juice of 2 lemons
40 g/1$\frac{1}{2}$ oz sugar (omit if bottled orange is used)	3 tablespoons sugar (omit if orange drink is used)
strips of cucumber peel	strips of cucumber peel
300 ml/$\frac{1}{2}$ pint port	1$\frac{1}{4}$ cups port
2 syphons soda water	2 syphons soda water
225-350 g/8-12 oz fresh fruit in season: strawberries, cherries, peaches, pears or apples	$\frac{1}{2}$-$\frac{3}{4}$ lb fresh fruit in season: strawberries, cherries, peaches, pears or apples
sprigs of borage and/or lemon thyme	sprigs of borage and/or lemon thyme

In a bowl mix the Burgundy, sherry, liqueur (if used), orange and lemon juice, sugar and strips of cucumber. Chill.

Just before the guests arrive, mix in the port and soda water. Place whole small fruit or sliced larger fruit in the bottom of the requisite number of jugs. Pour in the liquid and distribute the cucumber equally. Float the herb sprigs on top of each jug.

Spiced Peaches (see page 89)

Egg Ginger Warmer

This is a splendid drink for a frosty morning or as a nightcap. The cognac is optional but highly recommended.

METRIC/IMPERIAL	AMERICAN
3 eggs	3 eggs
2 tablespoons ginger syrup	3 tablespoons ginger syrup
2 ginger nuts, crushed	2 gingersnaps, crushed
450 ml/$\frac{3}{4}$ pint milk	2 cups milk
2 tablespoons cognac (optional)	3 tablespoons cognac (optional)

Beat the eggs, syrup and ginger crumbs together. Heat the milk until very hot but not boiling, and beat into the egg mixture. Stir in the cognac and serve immediately.

Mulled Cider

MAKES 6 GLASSES

In the United States, 'cider' usually means pure apple juice with no alcoholic content. This is an American recipe and therefore is non-alcoholic, but ordinary fermented cider may be substituted. If a stronger drink is desired, there is nothing nicer to my mind than vintage apple wine.

METRIC/IMPERIAL	AMERICAN
65 g/$2\frac{1}{2}$ oz soft brown sugar	5 tablespoons (firmly packed) soft brown sugar
$\frac{1}{8}$ teaspoon salt	$\frac{1}{8}$ teaspoon salt
$\frac{1}{4}$ teaspoon ground cloves	$\frac{1}{4}$ teaspoon ground cloves
$\frac{1}{4}$ teaspoon ground allspice	$\frac{1}{4}$ teaspoon ground allspice
$\frac{1}{8}$ teaspoon grated nutmeg	$\frac{1}{8}$ teaspoon grated nutmeg
2.5-cm/1-inch stick cinnamon	1-inch stick cinnamon
1.15 litres/2 pints bottled apple juice	$2\frac{1}{2}$ pints bottled apple juice

Mix the sugar, salt and spices in a saucepan. Stir in the apple juice, bring to the boil and simmer gently for 10 minutes. Strain through muslin and reheat when required.

Cider Cup

SERVES 12

For a delicious yet reasonably priced party drink, try this recipe. Make it with vintage apple wine or champagne cider for best results, or with any other cider for a less potent drink.

METRIC/IMPERIAL	AMERICAN
1 orange	1 orange
1 lemon	1 lemon
1 (339-g/12-oz) can pineapple chunks	1 (12-oz) can pineapple chunks
300 ml/$\frac{1}{2}$ pint dry or medium sherry	$1\frac{1}{4}$ cups dry or medium sherry
3 (775-ml/26-fl oz) or 4 (600-ml/20-fl oz) bottles cider	approx $2\frac{1}{2}$ quarts bottled cider
600 ml/1 pint soda water	$2\frac{1}{2}$ cups soda water
12 maraschino cherries (optional)	12 maraschino cherries (optional)
sprigs of mint and/or borage	sprigs of mint and/or borage

Peel the orange and lemon thinly and turn the zest into a large bowl with the juice of both, the contents of the can of pineapple and the sherry. Chill.

When ready to serve, pour over the chilled cider and soda water. Pour into jugs and add cherries and a sprig of mint and/or borage to each.

Index

Useful Facts and Figures

Notes on metrication

In this book quantities are given in metric and Imperial measures. Exact conversion from Imperial to metric measures does not usually give very convenient working quantities and so the metric measures have been rounded off into units of 25 grams. The table below shows the recommended equivalents.

Ounces	Approx. g to nearest whole figure	Recommended conversion to nearest unit of 25
1	28	25
2	57	50
3	85	75
4	113	100
5	142	150
6	170	175
7	198	200
8	227	225
9	255	250
10	283	275
11	312	300
12	340	350
13	368	375
14	396	400
15	425	425
16 (1 lb)	454	450
17	482	475
18	510	500
19	539	550
20 ($1\frac{1}{4}$ lb)	567	575

Note: When converting quantities over 20 oz first add the appropriate figures in the centre column, then adjust to the nearest unit of 25. As a general guide, 1 kg (1000 g) equals 2.2 lb or about 2 lb 3 oz. This method of conversion gives good results in nearly all cases, although in certain pastry and cake recipes a more accurate conversion is necessary to produce a balanced recipe.

Liquid measures

Liquid measures The millilitre has been used in this book and the following table gives a few examples.

Imperial	Approx. ml to nearest whole figure	Recommended ml
$\frac{1}{4}$ pint	142	150 ml
$\frac{1}{2}$ pint	283	300 ml
$\frac{3}{4}$ pint	425	450 ml
1 pint	567	600 ml
$1\frac{1}{2}$ pints	851	900 ml
$1\frac{3}{4}$ pints	992	1000 ml (1 litre)

Spoon measures All spoon measures given in this book are level unless otherwise stated.

Can sizes At present, cans are marked with the exact (usually to the nearest whole number) metric equivalent of the Imperial weight of the contents, so we have followed this practice when giving can sizes.

Oven temperatures

The table below gives recommended equivalents.

	°C	°F	Gas Mark
Very cool	110	225	$\frac{1}{4}$
	120	250	$\frac{1}{2}$
Cool	140	275	1
	150	300	2
Moderate	160	325	3
	180	350	4
Moderately hot	190	375	5
	200	400	6
Hot	220	425	7
	230	450	8
Very hot	240	475	9

Notes for American and Australian users

In America the 8-oz measuring cup is used. In Australia metric measures are now used in conjunction with the standard 250-ml measuring cup. The Imperial pint, used in Britain and Australia, is 20 fl oz, while the American pint is 16 fl oz. It is important to remember that the Australian tablespoon differs from both the British and American tablespoons; the table below gives a comparison. The British standard tablespoon, which has been used throughout this book, holds 17.7 ml, the American 14.2 ml, and the Australian 20 ml. A teaspoon holds approximately 5 ml in all three countries.

British	American	Australian
1 teaspoon	1 teaspoon	1 teaspoon
1 tablespoon	1 tablespoon	1 tablespoon
2 tablespoons	3 tablespoons	2 tablespoons
$3\frac{1}{2}$ tablespoons	4 tablespoons	3 tablespoons
4 tablespoons	5 tablespoons	$3\frac{1}{2}$ tablespoons

An Imperial/American guide to solid and liquid measures

Solid measures

IMPERIAL	AMERICAN
1 lb butter or margarine	2 cups
1 lb flour	4 cups
1 lb granulated or castor sugar	2 cups
1 lb icing sugar	3 cups
8 oz rice	1 cup

Liquid measures

IMPERIAL	AMERICAN
$\frac{1}{4}$ pint liquid	$\frac{2}{3}$ cup liquid
$\frac{1}{2}$ pint	$1\frac{1}{4}$ cups
$\frac{3}{4}$ pint	2 cups
1 pint	$2\frac{1}{2}$ cups
$1\frac{1}{2}$ pints	$3\frac{3}{4}$ cups
2 pints	5 cups ($2\frac{1}{2}$ pints)

NOTE: WHEN MAKING ANY OF THE RECIPES IN THIS BOOK, ONLY FOLLOW ONE SET OF MEASURES AS THEY ARE NOT INTERCHANGEABLE.